LEABHARLANNA FHINE GALL
FINGAL LIBRARIES

Items should be returned on or before the given return date. Items may be renewed in branch libraries, by phone or online. You will need your PIN to renew online. Fines are charged on overdue items. Damage to, or loss of items, will be charged to the borrower.

All the Time
We Thought We Had

A Memoir

Gordon Darroch

First published in Great Britain in 2018 by Polygon,
an imprint of Birlinn Ltd.

West Newington House
10 Newington Road
Edinburgh
EH9 1QS

www.polygonbooks.co.uk

1

ISBN 978 1 84697 447 2
eBook ISBN 978 0 85790 022 3

British Library Cataloguing in Publication Data
A catalogue record for this book is available on request
from the British Library.

Typeset by 3btype.com

Printed and bound in Great Britain by Clays Ltd, Elcograf S.p.A.

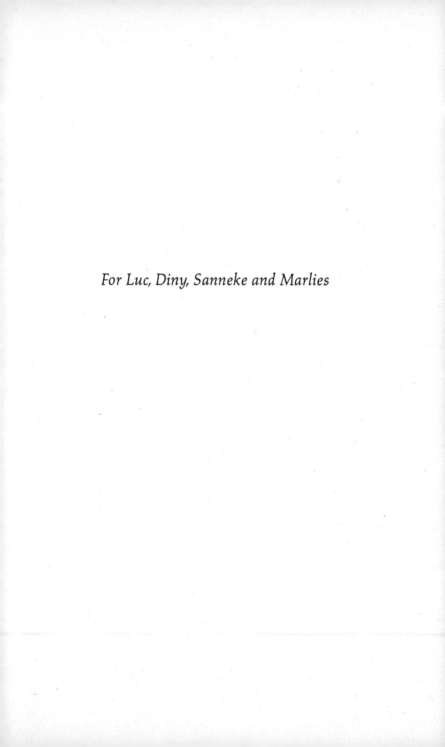

For Luc, Diny, Sanneke and Marlies

'Emotion, which is suffering, ceases to be suffering as soon as we form a clear and precise picture of it.'

BARUCH SPINOZA, *Ethics*

'So what if I die. Let me discover what it is that I want and fear from love.'

GILLIAN ROSE, *Love's Work*

Part One

Glasgow

Part One

Glasgow

1

When the world collapses it is not with a great blast of energy, like a tsunami or a fireworks display; it simply crumbles into dust. I discovered this brutal truth on my thirty-eighth birthday, when I sat with my wife in a small whitewashed room and heard a sentence that dispatched us to the worst place in the universe.

It was a bright late August day in Glasgow in 2012. I was working in the afternoon, so Magteld and I planned to go out for lunch. We would go to a café and have something with chips, in the good auld Scottish tradition. We would celebrate life and good health and contemplate the future, which glowed enticingly just beyond the horizon. Like good middle-class couples we were engrossed in our personal goals, the most immediate of which was to move to her native Netherlands. We lacked nothing materially, but in that way peculiar to people in the Western world approaching middle age we had a nagging sense that we were lagging behind ourselves. We needed to *get on*. Life was neither dazzling nor disastrous, and in any case there was still plenty of time for a fresh start.

And we were in unblemished health. Ordinarily that would have been an unqualified statement. But three months earlier a lump had appeared in Magteld's right breast. It appeared quite suddenly, hard and round like a golf ball, and firmly lodged. Her breasts were small, and there was no way, surely, that an incongruent mass could have squatted there unnoticed for long.

It was probably a cyst, the GP reassured her, but just to be sure he arranged for her to have an X-ray at the oncology department at the Victoria Infirmary. The words 'oncology' and 'radiographer' were jarring notes from a sinister realm that would resonate for months. We went on holiday to France and did our best to shut out the loitering sense of dread.

Thick clouds hung low during our two weeks in France. In the first week, on a campsite outside Gérardmer, we were ambushed by a mountain storm that smacked against the walls of our chalet and turned the stream flowing past the door into a fizzing torrent. When the clouds parted we went out and behaved as tourists do, walking along forest trails, eating in cafes, visiting museums where we knew nothing of the history, or paddling in the nearby lake. Holiday time constantly needs to be pushed forwards, in contrast to regular time which drags you along so fast you can feel your heels burning on the ground. One morning I rose early, inspired by Hemingway's dictum about mountain-tarn swimming, and traversed a smaller lake further up the hill. When I got out I noticed two things: a sign saying 'natation interdite' and the sharp gravel lining the path that led back along the lakeside to the spot where I'd left my shoes. Every jabbing step felt like a pinch of retribution for my illicit swim.

Euan and Adam, our two sons, spent much of the week paddling in the rushing stream, the icy water pouring over their bare feet as they scoured the water with their fishing nets for imaginary creatures. On the brightest day, we ventured out onto the lake in a pedalo while the locals sat huddled in the beach café looking as if the sky was about to fall on their heads. And all the while we tried to banish the thoughts of what was looming when we returned and time resumed its normal cycle.

Magteld could turn minor worries – a lost bank statement, a missed appointment or an unpaid bill – into full-scale crises. In Scotland she was called up several times for jury service. Each time, she phoned the court, obtained a doctor's note and sent it off with a cover letter explaining, regretfully, that her civic duty was incompatible with the demands of being a mother of two young boys with autism. For weeks afterwards she drove herself frantic with the conviction that some oversight or official intransigence would trigger a tyrannical sanction. Only once we moved to the Netherlands and I encountered the armoured fist of Dutch bureaucracy did I appreciate that this anxiety was not altogether rootless. Yet when a genuinely appalling situation arose she handled it with remarkable calm. Worrying wouldn't hasten the news or soothe the pain of waiting, and, anyway, it was probably just a cyst.

We spent the second week of our holiday in a large house in the Vosges, where her parents had invited the family to celebrate their fortieth wedding anniversary: three daughters, their husbands and the four grandchildren. Magteld's youngest sister, Marlies, had to call off when it turned out her first baby was due around the same time. The family gathering was upstaged by the fringe drama that the two daughters carried within them. The haze of uncontrolled events hovered on the horizon.

Magteld felt the distance from her family most keenly at birthdays. As children began to appear, these occasions became more frequent and livelier, and her sense of separation weighed heavier. I would watch her head dip, even as she made the effort to smile, as her mother reconstructed the scene over the phone. Visits to her homeland sometimes generated fanciful images in our minds of the brighter, happier family life we might enjoy there one day. We had consoled ourselves with the idyll of emigration for years, and made concessions such as giving the children Dutch middle names – Euan Hartger and Adam Floris. But it never went further than wishful talk.

It took the dull threat of cancer, that hard little lump, to turn our aspirations into something firmer. In France we discussed and developed our plans to move to The Hague, the city where Magteld's other sister, Sanneke, lived. We set ourselves a target of three years, before Euan started secondary school. It was daunting enough to raise two autistic children when we were in the prime of health, but how would we cope if one of us had an accident, or worse? I thought of the colleague's nephew who was killed one Monday night by a speeding driver as he left the gym, perhaps pausing to fumble for his keys in his pocket and wondering what to have for dinner in the seconds before the wayward car swatted him out of existence. Life was so fragile, so prone to random cruelties. The worst things we had imagined so far tended to be external: falling into a ravine, dying in a plane crash or walking round a corner and blundering into a knife fight. Cancer was a more intimate horror. It confronted us with the potential nightmares that lurk in our own bodies.

*

On another family holiday, six years earlier, in Normandy, we had seen some of the first clear signs of Euan's autism. Magteld's mother, Diny, took her grandson, then three years old, in his dungarees up to a field where he had seen some cows. He took her hand without a murmur and when he got to the edge of the field gazed at them blankly.

'Why don't you say anything?' Diny asked, in gentle exasperation.

Euan remained unmoved. She turned around, he took her hand again and they walked back down the hill.

Euan acquiesced in everything: if an adult held out their hand he took it with not a flicker of inquisitiveness. People reassured us he was a contented, placid child with an infectious, cackling laugh. 'I never hear him crying,' our next-door neighbour said approvingly. But at birthday parties we saw how other children ran around and chatted away, tasting language for the first time, while Euan stood and watched, seemingly disengaged, as if in a dream. His most familiar pose was standing in front of the radiator and singing songs memorised from his favourite CDs, running the words and instrumental sections into each other in a miasma of sound.

At nursery he played alone in the book corner. 'He's never any trouble,' the staff said to reassure us. One day a senior nurse was waiting for me when I went to fetch him. 'Let me show you something.' She laid out a row of numbered cards, in sequence, except for two of the cards. Euan immediately spotted the inconsistency and switched the misplaced cards. 'I've never seen a three-year-old do that,' she said, astonishment etched on her face.

'He'll be a maths genius,' friends said. But Euan was more of a puzzle than a prodigy: a quiet, almost eerily self-sufficient boy whose favourite pastime was watching the dial on the CD player. Friends and relatives told us he was too clever to be autistic. I know now that intelligence doesn't preclude autism. And 'contented' didn't explain the depth of his silence. Even when another child attacked Euan in nursery he didn't yelp or cry, and it was only much later in the day that one of the nurses noticed a large bruise on his face. Euan, however, had no words to explain what had happened.

We decided we must be doing something wrong. Magteld blamed me; I blamed her; we both blamed ourselves. We spoke for him too much, people said, unaware of the hours we'd spent waiting for him to reply. Magteld would shake and clench her teeth as she tried to compel him to listen. I bowed my head in passive rage. Once Euan was fixed on an objective he developed such pronounced tunnel vision that it became an agony to deviate from it. We made the mistake one Sunday of going for a walk in Queen's Park, where he liked to visit the snakes in the glasshouses. They were closed on Sunday, but Euan dragged me for a quarter of a mile by the hand, screaming his determination to see the snakes and only giving up, reluctantly, in front of the locked iron gates.

But autism? That was unthinkable. At the time the former doctor Andrew Wakefield was bent on convincing the world that the MMR triple vaccine was responsible for autism, and media coverage tended to focus on its most grotesque, distressing aspects. A typical news report would show a harrowed mother describing her withdrawn, emotionally frozen child, who could be seen in the background, sitting in a corner, rocking and flapping and emitting alien grunts, locked in their silent world. It was unthinkable that our bright, giggling, music-loving toddler could be one of these children.

We were frightened because we barely knew our son. We had a world to learn about him, and about ourselves.

*

Two weeks after our return Magteld went back to the hospital for the mammogram. 'It's probably a cyst,' the radiographer said as she fumbled the stubborn mass inside Magteld's chest. But just to be sure, she took a biopsy, a cutting from the lump, to examine under a microscope. The results would be revealed to us a week later. The appointment coincided with my birthday. So the lunch would be a double celebration, marking both my smoothly advancing years and our release from the fear of cancer that had blighted our summer.

We arrived at the clinic slightly before the prescribed time. It was the end of the morning session; only a few patients still needed to be seen, and Magteld was called almost immediately. We waited in the consulting room, all wipe-down furniture and shadowless light, for five merciless minutes. We joked about rummaging through the cabinets to see what we could steal. It was a way of not thinking about where we were, or why.

The door swung open and two women we had never seen before strode in. They were smiling cautiously. The room seemed to darken. I wondered why there were two of them, like detectives in a Sunday-night drama.

One woman sat down opposite Magteld, the other beside her, so that the four of us formed a diamond shape. The first introduced herself and her colleague. They gave only their names, not their job titles, I noticed.

In my memory this next scene plays out in slow motion, because I can scarcely bear to watch it through to the end. It was a moment when life spun on its axis, when the past and the future flipped polarities, like Alice stepping through the looking-glass: on the one side fear and missed opportunities, on the other hope and redemption. The conceit of youth is that the future is redemptive: there is always enough time to atone for past mistakes.

The surgeon, Miss Winter, is leaning slightly forward, ready to deliver her terrible payload. Her eyes are shaded, anticipating Magteld's response. The breast nurse, Jennifer, has her legs crossed and is tweaking her long dark hair. Magteld sits with her hands in her lap, her face cramped with fear. I am suspended in time, like an actor with stage fright, swamped with the desire to flee through a locked exit.

'I'm afraid this is a cancer that you have, Magteld,' said Miss Winter.

Magteld burst into tears. Horror flooded her eyes. She choked out a reply. 'I've got two kids. They're autistic. I need to be there for them.'

'We're going to treat it,' Miss Winter said immediately. She sketched out a plan in a language full of dissonant words: chemotherapy, mastectomy, radiotherapy, lymph nodes. The medical terms seeped out like toxic waste.

The treatment would take a year out of our lives. Instead of an alluring, hope-laden journey across the North Sea to the Netherlands we faced a year in hell, shuttling back and forth along a two-mile corridor across the south side of Glasgow between our house and the New Victoria Infirmary.

Jennifer brought out a book with a title like 'Explaining Cancer in Simple Terms to People Still Recoiling from the Abysmal Terror'. She went through it, crossing out passages with her pen: 'It's not that type,' she said as she marked a big X over one page. She flicked through again. 'It's not that type either, that's worse.' Vast sums of money had been spent on research to improve the prospects of cancer sufferers, she told us, in the manner of a car salesman describing the enhanced safety features of a family saloon. Then came the fine print. The chances of surviving had improved, but the outcome was far from certain. Tumours were inherently unpredictable. Cancer treatment was still, essentially, a crap shoot.

Later, as we sat in the garden in the glaring sunlight, eyes raw from crying, Magteld said, 'The stupid thing is, I don't feel ill. And yet I've got a life-threatening disease.' This is the awful cowardliness of cancer: it consumes you by stealth. It is a dumb, unfeeling thing, a bug in the DNA code. It is a silent mutiny within the body, terrorism by cell division, a populist uprising that destroys the system it depends on. Within a few hours of her diagnosis I hated it viscerally.

The phone calls began as soon as we got back from the hospital.

In Dutch, *kanker* is one of the ugliest words in the lexicon, the common root of its most venomous swearwords. It sounds harsher than its English equivalent: a pair of velar plosives to be spat out like rotten teeth. I had called off work so I could sit in the kitchen and hear my wife speak it, again and again, in between shrieks of despair, as she relayed the news to her family.

Nobody knew what to say. The callers expected inconvenient news at worst. Miss Winter had told us that even the consultants were surprised by the results. In the consultation room Magteld had turned to me, her eyes filled with tears, and tried a light remark: 'This isn't quite what we'd planned for your birthday.'

Jennifer, said, 'Oh, is it your birthday?' Until then I'd sat quietly, numb with shock, but now the tears streamed from my eyes. This was when I understood that this diagnosis wasn't just for Magteld; it would disrupt my own life, our children's and those of her family across the sea, in ways that we had barely begun to understand.

The treatment would take a year, and give us back the shattered pieces of our lives, if we were lucky. A year in hell, as if the plague sign had been painted on our door.

In this swamp of uncertainty and medical terminology, the question that consumed us most fervently was: *why?* Magteld was thirty-six and a half years old. She had had two children and breastfed them both. She had only smoked for a few months, when she was seventeen. The previous autumn she had taken up running. The only history of cancer in her family was her father's sister, who had been treated in her mid-forties and was still thriving a decade later. The biggest statistical risk was the fact we lived in Glasgow, but even that had only applied since her mid-twenties. Why had cancer sought her out?

We went to bed that night, exhausted and bewildered. As we drifted off to sleep another question took shape in the darkness: what on earth were we going to tell the children?

Maurice Sendak, a writer with a rare gift for understanding children, contended that they know everything. Hiding the truth from them, or trying to sweeten it, was not only dishonest: it was futile. Or as he put it more pithily: 'I refuse to cater to the bullshit of innocence.' Adults claim they lie to children to protect them, when their real motivation is to shield themselves from the searing curiosity children display when they uncover an unpleasant truth.

When Magteld dropped Adam off at school on the morning she was diagnosed, he refused to leave her side. He clung to her like ivy to a tree and only let go when the deputy head came out to lead him away. The startling thing was that she hadn't told him about the appointment. 'I'm clearly not a very good actress,' she observed.

After her biopsy she told the boys they would have to cuddle her on the left side from now on, because the other side was too sore. That night they moved into her bed, displacing me to the spare room.

Two hurdles stood in our way: what to tell them, and how to be certain they had understood it. Euan was nine, Adam on the threshold of seven. We couldn't be absolutely sure they knew what death meant. We started by talking about sickness, since they knew about that. I told Adam his mummy was going to be very sick for a long time, but that it was all to help her get better. He nodded silently.

Then I spoiled it by telling him he needed to be a good boy and not kick up a fuss. Which to an autistic child means: forget yourself. Be someone else. Climb on your own head. Do not exist.

Adam spent the next few days in a temper that wouldn't have disgraced a rhinoceros. One day I bought a wall clock for his bedroom. When I came home at the end of the day it was lying in pieces on the kitchen worktop, its hands frozen and a great crack splayed across its face. The clock face only showed the hours of 3, 6, 9 and 12, and the missing numbers had driven him to distraction, Magteld explained.

Gathering a small army of cuddly toys, he occupied my half of the double bed. Because Adam struggled to speak he gave away few clues about what impact his mother's illness had on him, but as her treatment went on, and her hair vanished, he became increasingly reluctant to go to school in the morning.

One day he managed to distil his anxieties into an explanation. 'I don't want you to take me to school because you're sore,' he said.

Magteld sat down with Adam and his toy reindeer, Finlay, so called because his grandparents had bought him in Finland.

'Why doesn't Adam want to go to school, Finlay?' asked Magteld.

'He thinks you're a different mum,' replied Adam, in Finlay's voice.

Adam's visual sense dominated his reasoning. He had watched from the bath as Magteld ripped her hair out in clumps, chortling at the spectacle, but when he realised it was gone permanently, he decided it must have been painful.

'But I'm still the same mum as before,' Magteld told Finlay. 'I just don't have my hair. And when I get better, it will grow back.'

That eased Adam's fears about the school run, but there were other tears in the fabric. I had fallen into the habit of using Magteld's illness to reproach him. Cancer had become a kind of third parent, a sullen and demanding stepmother. If he made too much noise in his bedroom while Magteld was sleeping next door, I told him to stop disturbing her. One morning I pulled the trick once too often and Adam yelled at me in anguish. For the first time I saw her illness from his point of view. A seven-year-old boy was seeing his strong, dependable mother transformed into a frail and hairless woman. He was grieving the loss of the mum he had known. And my response was to wrap his grief in my own anxiety and throw it back at him.

I stopped chastising him. I said his mum was trying to get better and he could help her by doing more for himself. His rage abated. But as Magteld's illness progressed, it became clear that Euan and Adam were terribly, terrifyingly aware of how grave her situation was. As Maurice Sendak argued, adults who try to protect children from bad news succeed only in deceiving themselves. We had no choice. We had to take them with us on the journey. We had to tell them the truth.

On the weekend after Magteld's diagnosis we went to Paisley for a picnic with a carers' group. It was a capricious September day, grey and sharp, with heavy clouds trudging across the sky, but for a few hours they rolled aside and the children played in the sunshine. There was a boating lake with a miniature railway that looped around it, and Euan and Adam spent most of the afternoon going round the loop, enthralled by the shriek of the train's whistle and the trundle of the carriages. Every so often Magteld ducked away to talk to a friend and returned, her eyes moist and a quiet smile of relief on her face. At this stage her diagnosis was still restricted to close friends, like pregnancy but without the joy.

As the weeks went by, the news rippled outwards to neighbours, distant relatives, acquaintances, colleagues and employers. Cancer, cancer, cancer: every repetition of the word stung like those stones on the gravel path in Gérardmer.

The reactions varied widely. Some elected to dispense cheap advice – 'stay positive' was a recurring platitude, as if we could somehow think the cancer into going away. Friends in medical professions had the unfortunate habit of saying things that were meant to ease our worries but instead contrived to add to them: one doctor asked, 'Is it positive?' Not only did I have no idea, but I was only just learning that there were as many different cancers as there are trees in the jungle, and the chances of us emerging from the thicket alive seemed infinitesimal. Most of all we came to dread that declaration of uncommitted support: 'If there's anything I can do,' usually combined with a flap of the hands as the speaker began retreating at a canter. We were glad of all offers of help, but we simply had no energy to do people's thinking for them.

There were the constant enquiries about Magteld's health. 'How are you feeling?' becomes a loaded question when it is asked dozens of times a day, in all circumstances, often paired with an expression of dramatic concern. Magteld would find it tagged to Facebook posts about the children's achievements at school, or her holiday photographs, or the weather. Every time she tried to forget that she was living through the nightmare of cancer, those four words would drag her back in.

But many people gave freely, even if it was just twenty minutes of their time for coffee and a chat. One friend appeared unbidden on the doorstep one evening with two Tupperware boxes full of frozen leftovers. Another offered to pray for me. In other circumstances I might, as a devout atheist, have dismissed or scorned such a gesture, but I welcomed it, because it acknowledged and valued our sense of vulnerability. The straight answer was no, there was nothing anyone could do to banish the pain, but every act of kindness made us feel a little less alone.

Now that we had entered the realm of cancer treatment the programme lurched forwards at harrowing speed. Magteld was diagnosed on a Thursday; on Monday she returned to the hospital for a second biopsy. The surgeons needed to carve a larger chunk from her tumour so they could probe the growth for clues about how to quell it. They would inject a radioactive dye to track the progress of the cancer cells. The operation would be done under general anaesthetic, Magteld's first since childhood, and the implication – of being slashed and stitched while she lay unconscious, and the faint chance she might not wake up again – pestered her.

'You're worried because you're healthy,' I said. 'People who spend their lives in hospital don't think twice about being poked and prodded.'

We had been warned that the rhythm of our lives would

have to submit to the chemotherapy cycle. Our well-being, our social lives and our capacity to care for ourselves all depended on how Magteld's body responded. The hospital appointments were inked in the diary, every three weeks until New Year, like breakwater posts stretching out to sea.

The advice was to use the good days and weather the bad ones. 'It's like I'm living my life in snippets,' said Magteld, and once again I marvelled at her dexterity with her second language.

When we arrived at the hospital on Monday we discovered the operation had been put back to the afternoon. Magteld sat and chatted with a fellow patient in the waiting room. I went home and had lunch in the garden, joined by a wasp that stung me between the fingers as I swatted it away. I yelped with pain, then instantly thought of Magteld lying, prone, on the operating table as surgeons grappled with the dumb assassin inside her. What was a wasp sting compared to that?

It was early evening by the time she was ready to be picked up. She was sitting up in bed, relieved and weary and in some discomfort from the operation. I helped her out of the flimsy dressing-gown she had bought from Marks & Spencer the day before, and pulled her cotton top carefully over her bruised arm. Over the next two years I would become adept at this kind of nursing work, but right now I was clumsy and hesitant, and she winced as I pulled down the sleeve.

'Just before I woke up I had a lovely dream,' she said. 'I was walking in the sunshine with the boys.'

'Was I there?' I asked selfishly.

'Of course you were,' she said with a soft smile.

At home we lay in bed, side by side, unable to clinch because she was too fragile, like a porcelain vase.

2

We met in Italy, two decades earlier. It was probably the only moment our lives could have crossed. I was eighteen and had a summer job with a company that hired campsite couriers to work all over Europe. Chance dumped me in the hills above Lake Garda, where every morning I rolled up the awning of my tent and drank in the view of the dazzling sheet of water cradled by vine-clad mountains. As I remarked in Magteld's eulogy two decades later, who could have failed to fall in love in such seductive surroundings?

The campsite was owned by a Dutchman, and many of the guests were from his homeland. The Dutch seemed to be the ideal folk to hang out with on holiday: relaxed, self-assured, accomplished drinkers and footballers, with a high proportion of lissom blonde girls, even if their language sounded more gargled than spoken. On the pitch across from me was Jacco, a Dutchman in his late twenties with a deep tan, a javelin-thrower's physique and a tentative resemblance to Sting. He worked campsites in summer and ski resorts in the winter, in a seamless hedonistic cycle. He seemed to me to be dazzlingly mature and wise, especially around women. That impression was cemented when he seduced his area manager within a few weeks and indulged in a raucous all-night coupling in one of the tents.

One day Jacco was standing by my tent when he pointed at two girls walking along the path below us. 'See those two Dutch girls over there?' I remember him saying. 'You should go and talk to them. I think the taller one likes you.'

The taller one was Magteld. She was seventeen and on holiday with a schoolfriend. I have a picture of her at that time, as slender as a reed, with blonde hair like silk draped over her shoulders, and legs of unblemished marble. She wears knee-length Lycra leggings, a tight-necked T-shirt adorned with a silver chain, and an air of impishness. She craned her long neck forwards as she walked and had a slight bounce in her step, and my first memory is of her twisting her head back over her right shoulder, fixing her pale blue eyes on mine and breaking into a shy smile. It's almost certainly a composite image, but that's how I remember the first time my eyes met my wife's, in the first week of June 1993.

Our first date was in the campsite bar, down the hill from my tent, overlooking the lake. It was early June, and the lights of boats flickered beneath us in the lingering twilight. I don't remember what we drank, or what we talked about. Probably Jacco and Magteld's schoolfriend were with us, and

Marco, the campsite watchman, and his girlfriend Roberta, who spoke better German than English.

On the walk back up the hillside Magteld's fingers interlaced with mine. We swung our arms together forcefully, keeping step as we climbed up the steep, dimly lit path. I had never kissed a girl before and wondered what the inside of her mouth would feel like. I had an inkling I wouldn't have to wait long to find out.

But that first night she simply said goodnight, lingering for a second on the edge of my tent pitch before retreating to her caravan. I was too good at waiting, it seemed. The next night the routine was much the same: the drink, the lake, the warmth of her slender hand as we walked up the hill. But this time, when we stopped at my tent, she took another four steps to the doorway and launched into a full-on kiss. I was so stunned I forgot to breathe for a second, like a novice swimmer, until her tongue enticed mine to dance. Her eyes were closed; mine were open and focused on the tiny frown on her forehead.

She went home after three more nights of those hastily snatched kisses. They seem rather coy in retrospect, sweet weightless souvenirs of a holiday romance. Magteld, her schoolfriend and her friend's parents drove back through the night to north-east Holland; to me it could just as well have been the moon. As they left I focused on the back of her blonde head through the window of the vanishing car, believing it was the last I would ever see of her.

Not once in all those sultry nights above Lake Garda had I dared to speak her name out loud. Magteld – a soft Dutch 'g' rolling into a solid 't' like a wave crashing against a breakwater – proved too much for my reserved English tongue.

By the next evening I was already consigning her to memory when the phone rang. The campsite staff shouted up to my tent from the cabin that served as their office, and I scrambled down the grass bank to listen to her voice, as sweet and fresh as honeyed tea. The night after that she called again. Letters followed in the next few weeks, since phone calls were expensive and had to be rationed. It's hard to believe now that at the end of the last century there was no cheap and easy way of making contact across an international boundary. Letters took a week or more to filter through the Italian postal system. Ours was perhaps one of the last truly epistolary relationships, when the anticipation of the weekly missive could make the most banal sentence seem to simmer with suppressed passion.

In those early months it was more like a pen-pal exchange than a traffic of billets-doux. A typical letter would begin with an observation about the weather, then summarise whatever had happened in the past week and close with a few plaintive sentences about how we yearned to be back in each other's arms. Perhaps I was charmed by her faltering English, which threw a veil of mystery over her personality; perhaps my mannered prose fostered the illusion that she was living through a Jane Austen adaptation. Whatever the reason, the writing habit survived the summer and, somewhat to my surprise, my first term at Edinburgh

University, and as the autumn wore on I made plans to visit Magteld in the week before Christmas.

I touched down at Schiphol airport on a Saturday afternoon. Magteld was waiting at the arrivals gate in a long black raincoat. Standing beside her was her father, Luc, a tall man in his early forties with sandy hair, a neat beard and an earring. With his crumpled leather jacket and jeans he might have been the manager of an up-and-coming rock band. We climbed into the back seat of the family Volvo, where a Tupperware box of cheese sandwiches and cartons of fruit juice had been packed for the journey across the Netherlands.

Even for a native of Norfolk, the Dutch landscape was astoundingly flat. Only the sky changed, fading from grey to a starless black, during the two-and-a-half-hour journey to Sleen, a one-windmill village near the German border in the province of Drenthe. 'We have some catching up to do,' I said, and clutched Magteld's hand for the first time since six months earlier on an Italian hillside. I had no real idea what to expect.

It rained for most of the week. We played board games, including chess, though not for long: Magteld was a poor player and an even worse loser. In the evenings we retreated to her attic room, beneath the deep pitch of the roof and the flat grey sky, with a platter of cheese and crackers. We met all four of her grandparents, who had lived through the wartime occupation and recently retired as farmers. It was the tail end of that time when contempt for a country that was a few hours' walk away ran through many people's veins like the poison of an insect bite.

When we lay in bed together Magteld's eyes glittered like stars, and her smile was a dazzling crescent moon. What this beautiful girl, with her porcelain skin and delicate breasts and irresistibly plump cheeks, saw in me, I wasn't sure. Our first attempt at sex was awkward and clumsy, and we sat on a bus the next day doubled up with leg cramp. That night we tried again, in the hope of expunging the memory, and thankfully with more success.

'I will never break our relation,' she said one evening, looking up at me with soft tears and a searching look in her eyes. I nodded, dumbly, and pulled her head against my chest. At the end of the week, as we parted at the airport, she removed the silver necklace from around her neck and draped it around mine. I boarded the plane feeling as if the textures of the world had changed: the damp air was keener, the soil thicker, the sea below restless and churning with life.

Easter, 1994. Clumps of daffodils and a canopy of thick white cherry blossom festooned the garden as Magteld visited my parents' home outside Norwich for the first time.

Our relationship had become a serious affair. I wore the silver necklace she gave me most days, and we were still writing each other polite, restrained letters once a week. She was working weekends, washing dishes in a restaurant kitchen, to save up for plane tickets to England.

In Norwich we strolled by the river, in the shadow of the giant cathedral. On a bend by an archway I stood still and waited for her to turn around. 'Why are we stopping here?' she asked, her eyes dancing, and I replied by clutching her waist and kissing her deeply. It was the type of impulsive act I had shied away from at Lake Garda, almost to my cost.

That summer her family went on holiday to England, Wales and Ireland. I picked her up from Shropshire, where her parents had booked a whitewashed cottage that could have been transplanted from a James Herriot novel. We took the train from Kidderminster, changing at Birmingham and windswept Ely, pottering through the black fields of the Fens, which must have seemed to her like an apocalyptic parody of her homeland. We went on days out to Cambridge, to the coast and all the landmarks of my childhood, but mostly we explored each other, in the garden or the seclusion of the attic, and by the time she went home, five weeks after arriving, we were inseparable.

From then on we saw each other at least every three months. Our romance required a lot of patience: a lot of my memories are of going for walks or reading in the garden. Once we were walking in the pine forest near her home among the *hunebedden*, Neolithic tombs of delicately stacked menhirs where early man had buried his loved ones, when a sudden downpour enveloped us. With nowhere to shelter we clutched each other and danced among the puddles, laughing and brushing wet clumps of hair from our faces as we kissed, and I tasted the cold rain on her apricot cheeks.

By Christmas of that second year Magteld was talking seriously about moving to Edinburgh. She had two years left at college; I had three more to go until I graduated. After qualifying she could come over for the summer and look for jobs in flower shops. She was determined in her quiet way, and although I worried she was acting on impulse, I knew we were at the point where our relationship had to take root or perish. We had probably spent no more than three months together, stretched out across three years. At some stage her family must have asked her if she was ready to take such a drastic step. But Magteld's will was as strong as a tethering rope.

In the summer of 1995 we went to Italy again, boarding a train in northern Germany and emerging sixteen hours later in Bolzano, where a mountain thunderstorm battered our tent for the first night. For the next nine days we backpacked round Bologna, Venice, Lake Como and Florence, bleeding every last drop from a ticket that allowed 3,000 kilometres' travel for a flat fare.

We saw much of the country through the windows of trains and hot, crowded buses, squeezing our rucksacks apologetically between the scowling passengers. These cities, and the Italian trains with their old-fashioned compartment coaches, were so familiar to me from family holidays that they felt more like home than most parts of England. To Magteld they were a novelty, and I relished playing the role of tour guide. I have a picture of her taken on the outskirts of Florence, at the midway point of our holiday and, as it transpired, her life, squinting and smiling into the sun with the Duomo rising up behind her. She wears a pair of loose linen trousers with an elephant motif she'd bought from a local market. I was entranced by the way they wrapped around her legs as she walked.

In Venice we stayed on the Lido, where we mocked the German campers' habit of bringing their alarm clocks with them, as if time always had to be marshalled, even on holiday. We found a tiny canalside bar, two streets and a bridge away from the main arteries pumping tourists through Piazza San Marco, and sat drinking Coke as the passing Venetians greeted the owner, a burly sallow-jawed man named Aldo. Later, as the light faded over the lagoon, we stopped in a secluded archway and kissed each other fiercely, the tang of seawater filling our nostrils.

In the years that lay ahead Italy would be a recurring reference point, the place where the tributaries of our lives had flowed into each other. One day, we vowed, we would return to Lake Garda, or spend a weekend in Rome, or go away to a hotel carved into a mountainside that we had seen in a colour supplement – perhaps when we had children, or for a special anniversary. It never occurred to us, as the night sleeper trundled between the black mountains and over the border into Austria, that we might never make it.

On 15 August 1996 Magteld's family stood in a semicircle in the living room of the house where she had been born, and which was still the only home she had ever known. Almost all her possessions were crammed into the back of my Renault Clio, which was parked outside, waiting to take us to the port at Hook of Holland and across the sea. On the other side awaited a job she had secured in an Edinburgh flower shop, a shared room in a student house and the great uncharted future.

Her mother, her two sisters and her father stepped forward one by one and took her in their arms. I stood a few paces back, giving them the space to cherish the last moments that Magteld belonged unambiguously to them. There were promises to visit, and to write letters and cards. When it came to her father's turn he spoke a single word, *meid* – girl – which succinctly captured the magnitude of the moment. She was leaving the family home, as an independent woman, to take on life with all its uncertainties. She had told me once she didn't believe in happiness. Now we had to make our own.

We got into the car, reversed down the driveway, gave a little toot and pulled away. A few seconds later she had left Sleen, within an hour she was out of Drenthe, and by nightfall she was on a boat, beyond the Netherlands and headed for a country she barely knew. I felt the burden of responsibility and the weight of hope, because I had persuaded her to cross a sea for me, but it would take me years to understand how or why.

3

Two days after receiving the biopsy results, Magteld met her oncologist for the first time.

Hospitals were still foreign territory; she had not yet accepted her place in the domain of the sick. We sat in a whitewashed corridor watching the patients shuffle by. An elderly woman bent at ninety degrees kept dipping her head up like a butterfly swimmer to check she was on course. Another woman, lost in the fog of dementia, was guided by a scowling nurse who said nothing apart from 'Come on', as if calling a petulant dog to heel. In the next corridor a man sat waiting, wearing only a hospital gown, his white legs glaring even through two layers of glass.

Dr Sophie Barrett's brisk manner was offset by a bright smile, which she deployed frequently to blunt the force of the messages she had to convey. She sketched out the plan in quick, clear strokes: chemotherapy every three weeks, for six sessions. Then a month's rest before the mastectomy. Then a month of radiotherapy. Then five years of medication.

Before that, though, Magteld's body would undergo a full audit: a bone scan to check cancer hadn't set up outposts in her organs, a CT scan and a heart scan to make sure she could endure the strain of the next four months. She would lose her hair, temporarily, and her breast, permanently, unless chemotherapy succeeded in obliterating the tumour. For the rest of her life she would be a cancer survivor. Her existence depended on the cancer remaining in remission and the compliance of her cells.

She complained she could hardly trust her own body any longer, and the suspicion was infectious. In bed at night I checked for lumps, asymmetric blotches, unexpected protrusions. I wondered about the pattern of moles on my back and scanned my nervous system for niggles of pain. The treachery of Magteld's cancer encouraged me to sense conspiracies everywhere.

Her rage boiled over in the sanctuary of the underground car park, after we had left Dr Barrett. 'This shouldn't be happening to me,' she spluttered, 'I'm not some old lady.' Disease and infirmity are callous intruders at any age, but to be ambushed by them at the age of thirty-six is brutal and appalling.

Magteld started writing a blog a week after she was diagnosed. She would not let cancer define or diminish her, nor flinch from describing the pain, weariness or trepidation. She posted a picture of herself on the chemo ward, bare-headed, lashed to a drip and smiling defiantly. She wanted to confront the myths that proliferate and choke any discussion of the disease. Like bravery: she didn't feel brave, just desperately unlucky. 'Brave' is a nod to the modern superstition that force of character can improve your survival chances. The terror of the disease is magnified by the tyranny of the fighting spirit. What doesn't kill you makes you stronger, goes the old lie. Nobody wants their friends to think that they died from not trying hard enough. We praise the cancer battlers for the same reason we once told stories of knights who slayed fire-breathing dragons: the need for heroes to banish our primal fears. But in doing so we deny them the need to be anxious, frightened, tired, resentful, angry and aggrieved.

She rejected the notion that cancer is the product of poor lifestyle choices, a modern echo of the belief that leprosy was a punishment visited on sinners by God. Cancer strikes mostly at random: living well does no more than tweak the odds in your favour. 'I live healthily,' Magteld wrote. 'Don't smoke, drink with moderation, keep fit by running regularly and eat a healthy diet. All I know is that it is not a lifestyle disease. If it was at least I could kick myself for having bad habits. And I'm allowed to feel angry that this is happening to me.'

In her first blog entry she asserted the right to be unhappy, and to be anxious: 'I can't stuff my anxiety away and make way for positive thinking at all times.' She dismissed the talk of bravery and fighting, and focused on the hard grind of treatment. Fighting confers a worthiness on the opponent, a misplaced sense of respect. But I didn't respect cancer. I hated this insidious, stealthy, unconscious killer that had subverted the mechanics of my wife's body. There was no question of a fair fight. Cancer needed to be flushed out by any means possible. Don't fight cancer, we said: fuck cancer. Fuck it to hell. Fuck it with a full-on chemical assault. Fuck it with weapons-grade radiation. Fuck it till your hair falls out and your nails turn yellow. Fuck it before it gets to fuck you.

Fighting is not a matter of choice; the will to live is irresistible, and the hard thing is to invest your hope in a gruelling and unpredictable course of treatment. We decided it was wiser to live in fear than delusion, because fear can be instructive. The most positive thought we held on to was that if she survived, we could start living again.

There was time for one last party before the chemotherapy began. My father was celebrating his retirement as a Crown Court judge with a marquee on the lawn. I was determined to persuade Magteld to fly down to Norwich, partly because it would be our last chance to travel for several months, and partly because the idea of spending a September weekend alone in Glasgow while the rest of the family availed themselves of some excellent champagne was too torturous to bear.

My parents' home offered us asylum from the regime of cancer. The boys could run loose in the garden while we dispelled the seeping fear by preparing for the party. Only close relatives would be told about her diagnosis, we agreed, to stop it gatecrashing the feast. It felt like the end of the belle époque, a last dance before the ballroom doors were padlocked.

My mother took Magteld into Norwich in the morning to buy flowers. Engaging Magteld's professional skills was a way of keeping anxiety at bay. During the biopsy ten lymph nodes had been removed from her arm, which had put an end to her career, since she no longer had any resistance to infections from plant scratches. She spent the afternoon gathering up rhubarb leaves and other greenery in the garden to fill the giant vases. I hauled the vases across the lawn and marvelled at her ability to conjure a magnificent display from such plain materials. Magteld, however, scowled and reproached herself as she worked to achieve the desired blend, like a musician who hears every wrong note in a recording.

The party began in the amber glow of a September evening. Magteld, fresh from an afternoon rest, was resplendent in a zebra-patterned dress. She was effortlessly beautiful and yet barely aware of it, sometimes to an aggravating degree. I could never understand why she got so apprehensive about social gatherings when she could make the room spin around her. When we excused ourselves to cook the boys' supper one of the guests chastised me: 'You can't take her away; she's the prettiest girl in the room.' In my memory she never looks so perfectly composed as she did then. As we walked across the lawn I wished time would stop long enough to let me indulge in the flash of her legs in the twilight, the softness of her voice, the warmth of her hand clutching mine.

The newly retired guests looked back over successful

careers and ahead to years of cruises, fine wines and indulgent lunches. They suddenly looked younger and more vital, like university graduates. Over supper my father regaled us with the tale of how his best man turned up at his wedding with a black eye: the two of them had gone camping in Germany and got into a fight over a girl. It was hard to know what was more incongruous: that these two punctilious lawyers had ever been in a fight, or in a tent, or that the versions of themselves in the anecdote were far younger than Magteld and I now.

The chemotherapy room was on the top floor of the New Victoria Hospital, with a large picture window that framed the tree-lined hillside of Queen's Park. In mid-September the trees were heavy with yellowing leaves and swayed gently in the breeze; as the treatment progressed through the autumn months their luxuriant crowns would become bare and scrawny.

Before the treatment could begin, Magteld had to sign some disclaimer forms in Dr Barrett's office, acknowledging, among other things, that she understood the risks of falling pregnant while her bloodstream was teeming with vivid poison. Then we went upstairs for the first of six episodes. Magteld settled into the soft blue chair, supported by two pillows, while a nurse eased the point of a needle into the back of her hand. Other patients sat quietly chewing sandwiches and reading magazines, or snoozed as the medication trickled into their veins from plastic bags. They had the demeanour of people dropping in to a church to pray.

Magteld and the nurse chatted contentedly as the syringe stealthily did its work. I headed for the café for a cup of coffee and a sandwich, away from the jungle of blood bags, drips and needles. By the time I came back up it was all over. Magteld greeted me with a faint smile of relief and apprehension. It was time to go home.

At first nothing happened.

Magteld fetched Adam from school at three o'clock, as normal. She made a cup of tea, read a magazine and watched the boys play in the garden. I cooked dinner. We sat and talked. Everything was eerily familiar.

At six o'clock she took her first anti-sickness drugs. The nausea came on like a sudden storm. The pain swept across her face, dulled her eyes and flushed her cheeks a hot shade of crimson. She threw up violently and took to her bed as a creaking fatigue seized her. Through the night her stomach rejected everything, right down to the slightest sip of water. She vomited, retched, dry-heaved, gasped, sipped at her water, vomited again. As she gasped for breath I ran shuttle relays to the bathroom to empty the bucket.

At about two o'clock in the morning I called out the emergency doctor. Magteld had been propelled so fast into the realm of the severely ill that her mind was still catching up. After the doctor's injection had calmed her recalcitrant stomach she sat up in bed and declared, 'I want to go for a run in the morning.' The doctor jolted in his chair, flattened his shirt front and suggested laying off the exercise for a while.

But Magteld was not to be kept down for long. By mid-morning, once the children were in school, she rose from her bed, though only for five minutes. She tried a banana, which her stomach immediately rejected. Later on she managed to keep down an apple. By the afternoon she could manage a whole sandwich. The next day she attempted a trip to the shops, ten minutes' walk away, and came back half an hour later, a bag of groceries in her hand and a look of triumph on her face.

Within a couple of days Magteld might have passed for a healthy person again. The reddish stain bestowed by chemo-therapy had faded from her skin, she resumed her daily walks and her hair seemed as sturdy as ever – so lush and firmly rooted that it was hard to imagine her deserted scalp. I lay in bed, inspecting her and looking for the first signs of it working loose. Her custom-made wig sat in a box on top of the chest of drawers, awaiting its debut.

The next Saturday night she stood in the bathroom pulling out clumps of dead hair as if it were candy floss. 'I'm like an autumn tree,' she said as she watched her disintegration in the mirror. 'It's oddly satisfying.' The sides receded first, then the top and finally the fringe. She concealed the effect for another week by wearing a hat and consoled herself in the meantime by shopping for headscarves on the internet.

Eventually it was down to a few wispy pale scraps – 'like a baby owl in spring,' she said. Impatiently she took the hair clippers from the drawer and prepared to excise the last stubborn follicles.

'Let me do it for you,' I said.

I ran the razor over her head until only a soft coating of stubble remained. It sharpened the outline of her face and helped the headscarves fit better.

The wig, however, was a disaster. It was similar to her own blonde shade, but a little fuller, slightly more honey-toned and with a hint of curl, giving her the air of a prim 1950s secretary. The craftsmanship was meticulous, right down to the flesh-coloured lining to make the parting more convincing.

She called her wig Connie. I took photos in the back garden, in the sunshine, attempting to show Connie off at her radiant best. Later that day Magteld went for a walk in the park. When she came home she had the look of someone who'd just been dropped off by an over-opinionated taxi driver. She and Connie were a good match, but the chemistry was wrong. Connie made Magteld's head sweat and itch, and at close quarters smelled faintly like a straw mat. A failed attempt to use her in the bedroom sealed her fate. Connie went back in her box, unlamented.

The real problem, Magteld told me later, was that Connie was too much like her own hair, and a constant reminder of what she had lost. Besides, the headscarves were a good deal more comfortable.

When Euan came home from school in the afternoon he would remove Magteld's scarf and rub her head. Sometimes he tried on her hat or her headscarves, and they laughed together. This little ritual was the way he processed the dramatic change in his mother's appearance. In the absence of language, the sense of touch, the feel of her scalp and the sensation of the soft turbans on his own head were his way of understanding the changes in her.

Euan was clinical in his approach, like a child who unscrews ballpoint pens to examine the spring mechanism. Hard facts were less intimidating than vague adult emotions. As Maurice Sendak observed, he knew everything, but lacked the words to tell us. After her biopsy he noticed the mark on her breast and asked what the doctors would do to her. It was rare for Euan to ask a spontaneous question, so clearly it had made a deep impression in his mind.

His school sought out some materials, and I found a comic book that used superheroes to explain cancer treatment. Euan barely looked at them. His attention was fixed on the retreat of her hair, the one change he could properly grasp and monitor. Once it was gone completely he asked me if it would come back when she was better. Yes, I said. But it would take until April.

Euan took out his diary, which had become his means of deciphering the world. He asked me, 'In April, when Mum's better, can we go to Hamleys?' We had scheduled a trip to the famous toy shop in October to buy a present for Marlies's baby, Tim, who had been born in July, but Magteld's hospital appointments had forced us to postpone it. Euan's question signalled a shift in his perspective: he could still look forward to the visit, even though six months must look to a nine-year-old like a Saturnine orbit. He opened his diary at 1 April and wrote: 'Mummy get better'. And then on 6 April: 'Go to Hamleys, find something for baby Tim'.

He grabbed his pen and spread the book open on the table. There was something else. Euan looked down at the blank page and said, 'In April, when Mum's better, will everybody be happy?'

I had no answer to that. Later I wondered: an earthquake can devastate a landscape and leave a beautiful ravine. Does that make it a happier place?

4

We thought we were being clever, having children early. Our generation tended to start families after securing a career and a home, believing health was a better measure than wealth of our fitness to raise children. Magteld's parents had settled down in their early twenties and were now enjoying walking holidays and meals in restaurants and afternoons when nobody cried, yelled, scrapped, wailed for lost toys or had to be taken to the playground. Still fit, still in their fifties and able to enjoy the company of their grown-up children. That would be us one day, we thought.

A year after we got married, Magteld was abruptly made redundant. Feeling worthless and marooned, she consoled herself by spending a week with her family in Holland. The morning after she returned she scuttled into the bathroom while I was still shrouded in the fog of half-sleep. Then the door flew open and she bounded onto the bed, and in that instant I connected the excitement on her face to the opened pregnancy testing kit on the bedside cabinet.

'You're going to be a dad,' she said, her eyes gleaming.

It was an uncertain time. For the first time since arriving on British shores five years earlier Magteld needed to find work, and pregnancy had just raised the stakes. But in that moment none of it mattered. We clutched each other fiercely and thought of nothing but the baby, this nameless bundle of cells drifting about her womb, and how it would swell and gain substance in the months to come.

*

Midway through her chemotherapy she spent a wet Sunday afternoon looking at pictures of breasts on the internet. Or, to be more exact, pictures of spaces where breasts had been. Though Magteld was distressed to lose her hair, she had the consolation it would grow back. Losing a breast would be permanent and more devastating. This act of life-saving mutilation was also a direct attack on her femininity. The right side of her chest would be a scarred stump of dead tissue. 'I've had some great times with my breasts; I'll be sad to lose one,' she said. I hadn't expected Magteld to mourn the loss of her erotic self in such stark terms. We never talked a great deal about sex. I made a clumsy stab at a joke: 'I love your breasts, but if I had to choose, I'd rather lose them than you.' The conversation flatlined.

She discounted silicone implants from the start: 'It won't feel part of me,' she said. Her treatment coincided with the off-putting revelation that some French cosmetic clinics had been using building-grade silicone in breast implants. Another procedure involved fashioning a false breast from fat tissue elsewhere in the body, but Magteld knew a woman who had been left in permanent discomfort by just such an operation. Cutting out a lump of fat, to her mind, would only compound the sense of mutilation.

The advantage of having small breasts was that Magteld had the option of wearing a 'softie', or silicone bag, tucked inside her bra. Perhaps she could have an implant later, once she had accepted her new shape, but she sounded unconvinced. Then she found a picture online of a woman with a double mastectomy sunbathing on a beach, two fine lines running across her chest. She looked elegant, not hideous or pitiable.

By her next visit to the breast surgeon, Magteld's mind was made up.

'What are we going to do about reconstructing you, missus?' asked Miss Winter.

'I don't want a reconstruction.'

'Are you sure?'

'Yes.'

Miss Winter checked Magteld's face for traces of doubt, saw that look of quiet resolve I knew so well, and nodded.

*

Our first home together was a room in a tenement flat on Edinburgh's Morningside Road, in the suburb that has become synonymous with Miss Jean Brodie, mothballed petticoats and 'you'll have had your tea' jibes. We, meanwhile, were living in sin, sharing a single bed in a student flat with no central heating and a kitchen window that jammed an inch from the top, so that when winter came we huddled together on the communal sofa in the kitchen, warming ourselves by switching on the oven and throwing the door open.

In December we moved into a one-bedroom flat on Nicolson Street which estate agents would call 'bijou'. The double bed almost completely filled one room while a three-piece suite took up about half the other, leaving just enough space to open the doors to the minuscule kitchen. Even the door at the foot of the cotton-reel turret staircase was too small to walk through upright. A few hundred yards up the road, though we were unaware of it at the time, J.K. Rowling was drafting the first chapters of *Harry Potter* in Nicolson's Cafe. We spent Christmas Day in that cramped space, carving the turkey on the coffee table before taking a walk along a deserted Princes Street, wrapping our coats together in a cocoon against the jabbing Edinburgh wind.

In Edinburgh she learned to dance. After graduating I spent a year in Preston, taking a postgraduate diploma in journalism, while Magteld chose to stay in Scotland. She took a room in a student flat and juggled working full-time in a flower shop with an undergraduate nightlife. Our relationship became long-distance once more, but she was more independent than she had ever been. Life was more austere when we moved together to Peterborough, where

I worked long hours as a junior reporter on the local newspaper while she cycled ten miles a day to work for a florist in Market Deeping. After a year we moved again, to Northampton, renting the upper half of an airy Edwardian house that backed on to the county cricket ground. In summer you could open the window and hear the crack of bat against ball, punctuated by the crackle of polite applause and the occasional strangled cry of 'Howzat!' My father, who was a fan of Northamptonshire, considered it idyllic, but we knew nobody in the town and loneliness began to cast its shadow. Our arguments became more frequent and bitter, and Magteld increasingly finished them by threatening to go back to Holland. I started to fear she meant it.

Gradually things settled. She signed up for driving lessons and started an Arts degree with the Open University. Her love of literature, art and music blossomed like a spring flower. For the first time in her life she felt valued for her mind and had an outlet for her natural curiosity. As a girl she had been diagnosed with deafness and had a series of operations to improve her hearing. She tuned out of lessons, cast adrift by her incapacity and the rigidity of the Dutch system, which took its revenge by sifting her into the lowest tier of secondary education. It equipped her with the skills she needed to run and administer a small flower shop, and this offered her a respectable living making neatly arranged bouquets for respectable people to place in their neatly arranged homes. Since leaving Holland she had had glimpses of a life that was less constrained, more unpredictable, more challenging, but more rewarding. As she focused on her studies, and passed her driving test, the threats to take the next boat home faded.

*

Cancer treatment is a black hole of exhaustion. It takes you to a level of fatigue that not even small children or all-night double shifts can match. The physical tiredness was exacerbated by extreme stress, mortal dread and, for Magteld, the Sisyphean exertion of chemotherapy. The drugs wiped out her white blood cells and weakened her immune system at the peak of flu season. The fear of succumbing to a virus gnawed at her, especially as a nurse at Adam's nursery had died of pneumonia while being treated for lung cancer. After her second chemotherapy session her doctor compounded the situation when he told her she was 'in no state right now to fight an infection'.

I was working two days a week and one weekend a month so we could make ends meet, and to give me a little respite from our cancer-infested house. That was until one damp, dismal Saturday in November, when Magteld called me up in the middle of the afternoon and begged me to come home. The merciless Glasgow rain was holding her hostage; she was terrified of catching a chill if she went out to the shops. I went straight home and cancelled my weekend shifts. We were withdrawing, having to slow down, which, as she reflected on her blog, is like cold turkey for the plugged-in generation:

It is hard to get used to resting when my mind is so active. I have had to learn to take time out and lie down with a book. Recently I started knitting as a way of relaxing. I learned how to knit when I was a child and I felt like taking it up again. It is another way to rest my active mind and concentrate on just one thing.

Leisure time no longer existed; concentration gave way to emotional numbness. I had been a keen 10K runner, but now I couldn't manage more than one training run a week. Magteld kept up the cooking and fetched Adam from school, but spent most of her remaining hours on the sofa, asleep.

Around the time I gave up the weekend shifts I had a dream about a race. I set off gently, aiming to conserve energy, but as the race went on I noticed myself losing speed. The more I tried to speed up, the stiffer and more sluggish my legs became. The sensation was like stirring a pan of thickening porridge. A much older runner shuffled past, grey hairs dangling from his legs. I tucked in behind and tried to keep pace with him up a hill, expecting to pass him on the downward slope, but my legs cramped up and he pulled away easily, his back shrinking as he melted into the distance. I felt angry and helpless, but the rage only constricted my movement more, until my knees could barely bring up my feet. I woke up, scared and sweating and bewildered. The seed of it was the dread of ageing, losing one's faculties and strength, the slow unravelling of the body's apparatus, all the things that were happening to Magteld at an accelerated rate, like a nuclear reaction.

Exhaustion crashed over us relentlessly. She was once reduced to tears because she was unable to squeeze an orange with a juicer. Another time our washing machine expired with a grinding, rattling sigh. I told her I'd mislaid a house key and wondered if it might be in the pocket of a pair of jeans which was now in the stricken drum. Marlies was visiting the following week with Tim, and the prospect of looking after a four-month-old baby without a working washing machine shredded the last scrap of Magteld's nerves. The row that followed swept away what little energy we still had. Two days later a repairman came out and diagnosed a worn-out mechanism. The door key turned up a few weeks later: one of the children had posted it behind a radiator.

*

We moved to Glasgow in the summer of 2000, having bought a flat on the top floor of a red sandstone tenement at the far end of the Great Western Road. The hallway had the kind of resplendent stone steps that chimed as you walked up them and a brass-studded banister kept scrupulously polished by the elderly widow across the hallway. Beyond Anniesland Cross the road ran out through Drumchapel, past the Clyde estuary and on to Loch Lomond, Glencoe and Inverness. The A82 was an umbilical cord that connected Scotland's natural heritage directly to our front door.

I went up to Scotland three weeks ahead of Magteld, commuting from Edinburgh until we were able to move into the flat. Sometimes I didn't get home until nearly midnight, which made me grateful it was midsummer. On a clear June night there is still a smudge of blue in the northern sky to guide you along the M8. On one of those nights, as the silhouettes of the Ochil Hills slid past the window, I made up my mind to ask Magteld to be my wife.

We had talked a lot about not marrying. It was old-fashioned and pointless. We were still in our mid-twenties. Our children would not suffer for being born out of wedlock. Marriage seemed principally designed to make separation more difficult. But there was no denying that we looked and behaved increasingly like a married couple. We had moved in step from Edinburgh to Peterborough to Northampton, and now to Glasgow. If we were to separate we couldn't simply vanish from each other's existences. Our lives were too entwined, the weight of shared memory too great.

I didn't go down on bended knee. I didn't buy her a ring. I still needed to pretend it was no big deal. When I went down to Northampton to rejoin her I simply stood in the living room and said, 'Hey, Mag, shall we get married?' She grinned and locked me in a deep embrace, and said yes, and I had the feeling that she had anticipated the question long before the thought had taken form in my mind.

✳

She made a point of walking the mile and a half to the New Victoria Hospital for her cancer treatment when she could. It helped her combat the weariness and worry, and escape the sense of living in a cocoon. On a sharp November morning we walked up together for her fourth chemo-therapy cycle. Once it was done she would be past the halfway point, and we planned to stop at a café on the way home to celebrate and fortify ourselves with tea and chocolate cake. Chemotherapy had degraded Magteld's taste buds and left a harsh, metallic taste and a parched sensation in her mouth. Favourite recipes, such as spicy lentil soup, were unpalatable; dry foods, such as bread, acquired the texture of sawdust. Eating had become a discipline instead of a pleasure, driven not by appetite but the need to keep her weight up. But she could always manage chocolate and cake, and appeased her tarnished palate with new flavours such as ginger beer. She consumed yoghurt, milk and cheese to stave off the danger of osteoporosis. And she looked forward to the treats of Christmas: a succulent turkey, mince pies and mulled wine.

I noticed how she hunched forward as she walked, and pulled her coat around herself. Lifting her knees had become an effort. On the steepest section of the route, a hill that rose steeply from the White Cart Water towards Queen's Park, she had to stop twice to regain her breath. Just a few weeks ago she had pranced up it on her weekly runs; now she had the gait and posture of a woman thirty years older. Time was warping.

The slower pace changed my perspective. On the way to the hospital I noticed how the south side of Glasgow was speckled with patches of thick greenery that could have been transplanted from the jungle. I thought I knew every inch of these streets from my weekly runs, but I had been moving too fast, and with too much purpose, to see the abundance of life on the verges.

*

On a damp September day in 2001, the kind when the fields shimmer with a veneer of rainwater, Magteld and I were married in the old municipal hall in Sleen. In the 1970s, when it was still a functioning government office, her father had been part of the living fabric of this building as a young Labour Party councillor; a century earlier Vincent van Gogh had tramped through this countryside on a dawn walk to the nearby village of Zweeloo, remarking on the church tower and admiring the 'tones of golden green in the moss, of reddish or bluish or yellowish dark lilac greys in the soil, tones of inexpressible purity in the green of the little wheat-fields'. Amid this suppressed, understated beauty, easily missed at first sight amid the overwhelming flatness and the upright conformity of the trees in their regimental straight lines, we pledged ourselves to each other in a plain civil ceremony, shorn of the theatrical language of Anglican conventions: for richer and poorer, in sickness and in health, till death us do part.

My kilt clashed vibrantly with the horizontal fields, less so with the flat grey sky, and nicely complemented the redbrick castle in the border town of Coevorden where we held the reception. We travelled there on an old red Routemaster with an open back door, an inspired choice by Magteld's parents, even if its rudimentary suspension was ill-equipped to deal with the Dutch fetish for speed bumps. Magteld wore a dress she had bought off the peg in a high-street store, in keeping with our insistence on downplaying the occasion, but she was too beautiful not to shimmer, even in the drizzle. Almost everybody we invited from Scotland and England had made the journey. It was an incongruous sight to see these people gathered in what I had come to think of as my Dutch country retreat, and together with our families they filled the Ridderzaal with the buzz of happy camaraderie.

The next morning I woke to find Magteld's side of the bed empty. She had slipped out early, feeling invigorated, and gone out on her bike to tour the village. Perhaps she wanted to see if the world had changed in the night, when a short intense storm had crudely interrupted us by flinging open the balcony door.

Our wedding day seems now to belong to a different age. One of our guests made everybody laugh with a story in the news about a man who had been stopped at airport security for trying to take a Welsh sporran through customs. We chuckled and shook our heads at this absurd display of pernickety officialdom; these were the days when you could arrive at the airport twenty minutes before departure time and still expect to get on the plane. Four days later we went to check in to a hotel in the French city of Troyes. The receptionist breathlessly informed us that *un avion touristique* had developed a fault and crashed into the World Trade Center.

'*À Amsterdam?*' I asked, parochially.

No, she replied: New York.

I switched on the television in our room and watched, for the first time, the now familiar images of a plane crashing into one of the Twin Towers in Manhattan. The other tower was on fire. Through the smoke I saw the decapitated remains of another plane sticking out of the side of the far tower.

That evening we sat in a cafe, watching the television and trying to decipher what had happened through the medium of my rusty French. In Paris the next day we saw armed guards at the railway station and met Americans who were scrabbling around trying to find hotel rooms because all the planes had been grounded. It gave the events of 9/11 a surreal, distorted quality. We learned the news in fragments, through the prism of a foreign language, as we floated on a plume of postnuptial bliss. Only when we drove back over the Dutch border four days later and reconnected with the known world did we really grasp how much had changed.

*

The poison cocktail was changed for the second half of Magteld's chemotherapy regime, and with it the side-effects. The sickness would diminish, but she was warned to expect aching joints and the thing she feared most: an increased risk of infection. There was also the possibility of an allergic reaction to one of the drugs, docetaxel, in which case the nurse would have to pump extra anti-allergens into her veins before 'rechallenging' her. The word made her treatment sound like a grotesque twist on arm-wrestling. The good news was that the reaction would happen in the first five minutes or not at all.

She sat back again in the soft blue chair. The trees outside, which had been thick with leaf when we first walked into the clinic, were swaying nakedly in the autumn breeze. The drip-feeding commenced. A slight dizziness overcame Magteld, but within ten minutes it had passed and she relaxed, knowing she had dodged the vomit trap.

All the nurses recognised her by now. They called her by her name and shared a joke as she sat on the drip. How could they be so unflappable, I wondered, when confronted by a constant stream of the grievously ill? The senior nurse glided around the ward with the air of a zen master in his soft slippers, dispensing instructions to his staff, pausing occasionally to check that the poisons were being administered correctly. How did it affect them to be the guardians of these people's lives, knowing as they did that many of them would be cut agonisingly short, despite their best efforts? How do you cope when existential dread becomes a feature of the scenery?

Unfortunately, she was a terrible patient. She resented the impositions of sickness and treatment, hated yielding to the instructions of doctors. She resisted the role of invalid to the stubs of her teeth. She tolerated sympathy in small doses, as long as it didn't remind her of her vulnerability. Anyone who tried too hard to lighten the load, or threw in an enquiry of 'How are you?' at an inauspicious moment, was met with a look of steely disdain.

She was unforgiving to herself when fatigue overcame her. 'I hate being this way,' she said. A kind of ascetic masochism was evident in her reluctance to take painkillers. Accepting the medicine meant first submitting to the pain when she was determined to conquer it. Persuading her to take a couple of paracetamol tablets could become a drawn-out negotiating process. It would pass over, she said; she didn't need the pills, she just wanted to get comfortable. Magteld worried that if she became reliant on painkillers it would soften her resistance. She preferred to fight the pain bare-knuckled. Only when every alternative had been exhausted and fatigue crept over her did she relent and take her medicine, and the storm was stilled.

One evening two of Magteld's closest friends asked if they could bring something round. She wanted to say no, but the eagerness in their voices when they phoned suggested this was more than just a casual visit. Half an hour later they arrived with a plastic shopping bag, which they opened to reveal a woollen bedspread, woven into coarse squares of forest green, cornflower blue and magenta. Over coffee her friends described how they had worked in tandem, crocheting the individual squares separately at home before knitting them together at the end. They synchronised their work in a carousel of phone calls over several weeks, like a resistance cell plotting an underground mission. The only reward they sought was the delight of a sick friend. When they unfolded it the fatigue evaporated from Magteld's face and for the next hour she laughed and talked animatedly, as if galvanised. I remember how she lay on the sofa on winter evenings wrapped in it, enveloping herself in the warmth and love that were threaded into the fabric.

Of all the things I inherited from Magteld, this symbol of friendship is among the most precious. When I take it out and unfold it at the onset of autumn, its muted shades trigger a stream of memories from those days. Perhaps there is still a trace of Magteld's scent snared in the wool. For a collaborative project the finished piece is remarkably harmonious, but I cherish all the little imperfections, because those are the places where its story (is that loose thread a relic of the moment someone rushed to answer the door; does this one bear witness to a shocking twist in a TV crime drama?) is written.

As Christmas approached, the damp of November sharpened into winter proper. The sky turned a piercing blue, frost was sprinkled across the ground and the cars in the street, and plumes of foggy breath bloomed from people's mouths as they spoke. Magteld felt more confident going outside in the bracing cold than in the mild, wet weather where she sensed disease in every droplet. One Sunday afternoon we went for a walk in Pollok Country Park. The half-hour stroll in amber-coloured sunlight, as the children zigzagged between the hedgerows and skated across frozen puddles, felt like a major excursion after weeks of being virtually housebound. Just being outside seemed liberating and challenging, a small victory for life. We would not give up; we would not forget. Here was the world, ready to welcome us back once our year in hell was over.

Not since childhood had I anticipated Christmas so keenly. After an autumn whose rhythm was a three-week cycle of deepening austerity, isolation and fear, the seasonal rituals gave us a much-needed focal point. My parents were visiting, and Magteld's treatment was nearing its end. In the first weekend of December I took the boys to buy a tree, carefully inspecting the stock for volume and needle retention. (Christmas-tree selection is an essentially male pastime, like barbecuing, and reflects the same obsession with technical specifications. Nobody considers 'leaf retention' when buying a beech hedge.) Later that week we went holly scrumping in the small park near our house, where the monstrous holly bush groaned with berries by mid-December. In the darkness of mid-afternoon we sneaked in with a pair of shears and clipped away a clutch of branches from around the back of the bush.

Christmas Day fell a week before her final treatment. Her aches and pains had eased enough to join us for what was, we hoped, our last Christmas dinner in Glasgow. After lunch she went back to bed, but she had participated, that was the main thing, and for a few hours we could remember what normal, unthreatened life felt like.

Former routines were creeping back in at the edges. Magteld was walking most days now and cooking when she could. I still did the shopping and the laundry, which Magteld resented in the latter case, since hanging out the washing had been a form of therapy for her. A carers' centre had arranged for a cleaner to come in once a week to give both of us some respite. And so we limped, like parched desert explorers glimpsing the oasis, into 2013.

5

Our home for the last seven years had been a roughcast red sandstone terrace house on Beaufort Avenue, typical of Glasgow's suburbs, with trapezoid bay windows to catch as much of the scant sunlight as possible. Magteld spotted it in the newspaper one morning, and though we felt no great urgency to move out of our ornate Victorian flat on the edge of Queen's Park, the pull of suburban living proved too strong. Euan was three years old, Adam nearly one, and we had acquired a new set of priorities, almost by stealth: docile streets, reliable schools, neighbours we knew by name, and a garden.

When we moved in, the house had a unkempt quality. The wood panelling and stained maroon carpet in the dining room gave it the air of an amateur rugby-club bar. The bathroom was a black-tiled cave equipped with a spa bath that wheezed and spluttered when I tried to make it work. All the light fittings had the bobble-ended switches that

I recognised from 1970s period dramas. The first three feet of lawn were a parched brown, a curious sight in the middle of a soaking wet September. When we first viewed it the previous owner sheepishly admitted that he had accidentally treated it with weedkiller instead of fertiliser.

We fashioned it into a home, one room at a time. We ripped out the wood panelling, pulled up the grotesque leylandii hedges that had sucked the daylight out of the neighbours' garden, rewired the electrics and gutted the bathroom. We replaced the lawn, uncovering a mass grave of broken bricks and rubble just below the surface, and Magteld took charge of the garden, planting a maple tree at the end and restoring order to the flowerbeds. After two years we converted the attic into a bedroom for Euan. Adam was inconsolable when his brother moved out, until he realised that it meant he had a room to himself as well.

Suburbia was rigid and unchanging compared to the transient life of the city tenements. It took time to acclimatise to the steadier pace, the boundary walls and picket fences, the roar of lawnmowers and hedge trimmers on a Sunday afternoon. But with two children soon to start school, it had become our natural habitat. Many of our neighbours had lived contentedly in the same house for several decades and knew each other better than their own relatives. When one of their daughters got married, the whole street turned out to wave her off on honeymoon.

It seems absurd now, but my greatest worry was that our love would perish in the stagnant atmosphere of suburbia. In fact we were on the brink of turbulent change. Both our children would be diagnosed with autism, emigration graduated from an aspiration to a matter of urgency, and cancer was about to emerge from the shadows to menace us. My fear that Magteld and I would fall out of love was grounded in a naive understanding of the word.

*

The start of 2013 brought dispiriting but not unexpected news from Dr Barrett. Magteld's tumour had resisted the firestorm of chemotherapy. Its shape had changed from a round pebble to something more like a pumice stone, but it was otherwise unscathed. The minuscule chance of her breast being spared was gone.

Magteld accepted the loss with mixed feelings. Her breasts had sustained the lives of her two children, but now one of them was threatening her existence. The operation was set for early February, giving her five weeks' respite before the radiotherapy started.

Her chemotherapy was concluded on 2 January, a public holiday in Scotland. Ordinarily the department would have been closed, but the cancer nurses came in for an extra half-day to deal with a backlog of patients. The mood was laid-back and cheerful, sprinkled with anecdotes of Hogmanay. Once Magteld was finished at 2 p.m., everybody went home. The ward had become a place of sanctuary. She knew the nurses like good friends by now; they had guided her through her treatment and given her quiet encouragement. They had talked to her, shared jokes and made her feel she was still a person as well as a patient.

We knew cancer was a percentage game. Consultants could offer prognoses and talk about likelihood of recovery, but the outcome for the patient is binary: you live or you die. Whether your chances of surviving are 5 per cent or 95 per cent, if you die you're still just as dead. And if 95 per cent sounds like good odds, transfer it to the context of a crowd of 5,000 people attending a concert, a political demonstration or a football match. If 250 of them die in an accident it's a disaster, even though 95 per cent of the crowd has survived.

The Victoria Infirmary was a grand old lady of a hospital: slightly aloof and intimidating, a gothic labyrinth with wide staircases and cavernous corridors. It was built on a steep hillside, round the corner from Queen's Park and next to the site of the Battle of Langside, where the deposed Mary, Queen of Scots made a last hopeless lunge for her old crown.

Magteld's mastectomy was booked for 8 February. She packed a hospital bag and a book for the waiting room, but when she arrived she discovered she was first in the queue. 'The good thing about it was I had no time to think,' she wrote on her blog:

> I talked to the anaesthetist and changed into a hospital gown and surgical stockings. When I was ready I was taken into the theatre, and when I woke up from the anaesthesia I looked down to see my breast was gone. I felt relieved, as I was finally rid of the tumour that has been a constant reminder of the cancer.

After school the boys and I went up to the hospital, where Magteld had bagged a single room on the cancer ward. She pulled down her top to reveal the tip of the scar beneath the bandages. It was a test, to see if I would flinch from the sight of her ravaged chest. All I felt was gratitude that the hateful, hostile tumour was gone, that I would never again have to feel that lump squatting beneath her skin.

The surgery was tidily done, but the skin around the scar was bloated and yellow. The boys peered at it for a moment, then went over to check out the commode in the corner of the room. She looked up at me and asked if she looked like a freak. No, I said, her life was more important. She smiled and kissed me, hesitantly.

She was outraged to find that the hospital had no fresh fruit, despite an abundance of vending machines stuffed with sugared drinks, crisps and chocolate bars. The next day I returned, laden down with apples, bananas, grapes and blueberries. I arranged them in a bowl and watched Magteld devour them like a famished jackal. I brought a bunch of flowers from the Valentine's Day selection and arranged them in a vase. It was a rare treat to be able to bring her Valentine's flowers, since in her old job she would stay up all night binding red roses to meet the demand for commercially ordained gestures of romance.

Magteld was impatient to be back home, with her boys, and eating the grilled salmon I'd promised for that evening. The doctor thought she should stay the night. He tried to persuade her, in that diligent manner peculiar to doctors, like a dog guiding sheep into a pen. She was free to choose, he said. The room was hers for as long as she needed. There were real concerns, too. During Saturday night her blood pressure had fallen so low that she collapsed on the commode. But she persisted. The best the doctor could achieve was a promise from her to come back and see the breast nurse in the morning.

By the time we visited the nurse, Magteld's chest cavity was pale and swollen, and she felt tired and uncomfortable. She was referred to the doctor and we waited in the canteen, trying to soothe our anxiety with coffee and shortbread. The doctor diagnosed a haematoma. The fluid needed to be drained immediately, before it went septic. That meant another operation, under anaesthetic, and another night in hospital.

Magteld was taken to a waiting room, while I went home and made up an overnight bag, in what was becoming a well-drilled routine. When the boys came home from school I had to tell them Mum was back in hospital. I bundled them, bewildered, into the car and we set off. But when I parked at the hospital and opened the car door Adam refused to get out. This new intrusion of his mum's illness had wrecked the version of events we had carefully constructed for our children. He wanted to see her at home, not in hospital, so he sat immobile, as if waiting for reality to blink first. If Maurice Sendak had been in the car he would have tutted and shaken his head.

When we finally got inside we found Magteld in the waiting room, wearing a surgical gown and looking pale and exhausted. She seized my hand tightly. Her surgery would be in the late afternoon. I could see from the boys' distressed faces that a full-scale meltdown was looming. I wanted to stay with Magteld, but she saw that they needed their routine of supper and bedtime. Go, her eyes said to me. I'll be fine. I kissed her and gave her a stack of magazines donated by our next-door neighbour, the kind that seem to be written specially for people about to undergo major surgery.

'Once they left I became very scared,' she wrote. I still shiver when I think what must have been prowling in her mind during those hours. The encroaching blackness, the whiff of the abyss. It was the first time, she told me some weeks later, that she had gone to sleep without the assumption she would wake up again.

After I had cooked and put the boys to bed, the hospital phoned. Magteld had come round from the operation and was recovering on the ward. We went to see her the next day, bearing more armfuls of fruit. Though she was visibly tired, some vibrancy had returned to her face. She had lost around a quarter of her blood and needed a transfusion in the night. The single room she had so avidly given up was no longer available, so she was in with a dozen other cancer patients. Nearly all of them were at least twice her age. Some had long lost their sense of daily rhythm, so the night was punctuated by the sound of bedside buzzers and nurses gliding softly through the ward.

She came home a week later. 'The sky has been blue for the last few days and although it is cold it feels as if spring is on the way,' she wrote. 'I'm more relieved than mournful about the loss of my right breast. The most important thing is I'm alive and able to enjoy life with family and friends.'

When Euan was three and a half, not long after the nursery staff had entranced me with his card-sequencing trick, the manager asked if an educational psychologist could come and observe him. I was vaguely stunned. I didn't know what an educational psychologist was, but it sounded ominous.

'Are you worried about him?' I said.

'A wee bit,' she replied.

I told Magteld. We were concerned but also relieved that someone else had noticed. Because in truth, Euan's habits weren't always so endearing. His speech development seemed to have stalled. His habit of singing by the radiator while his breakfast sat neglected on the table was setting us on edge. He responded to questions with blank stares or bypassed games of pass-the-parcel to absorb himself in the workings of the CD player. His days were built around obscure pernickety routines, and any deviation could precipitate a furious, limb-twirling rage.

Autism is unfairly blamed for wrecking marriages. Yet the seeping realisation that your child is fundamentally different has a coruscating effect on a relationship. Parenting is a middle-class bloodsport, and the sight of your child lagging behind in his development brings on feelings of shame and disappointment. Euan's autism placed an extra strain on a relationship that had started to fray. We blamed ourselves, and blamed each other. It was easier to believe that his behaviour was caused by bad parenting than accept that his brain was wired differently. Why did Magteld insist on replying for him when someone asked a question, without giving him a chance to speak? Why wasn't I taking him to sports clubs at weekends so he could run about with other boys?

The nursery manager said a formal assessment of Euan could take several weeks. In the meantime we decided to blunt the sense of helplessness by consulting a private therapist. I drove to her house and watched Magteld lead Euan inside a whitewashed bungalow halfway up a hill in Glasgow's genteel outer suburbs. When I collected them at the end of the appointment Magteld was standing in the doorway saying goodbye as Euan tugged at her hand. She walked to the car carrying a blue brochure and with a broken smile on her face. I noticed her eyes were moist. When she got into the car I saw the words Autism Spectrum Disorder on the cover of the folder. It was our first encounter with the term.

Magteld had burst into tears when the therapist pronounced, after watching Euan play for an hour, that he was almost certainly autistic. A full diagnosis would take months. We looked at each other in numb disbelief as Euan blissfully kicked his legs in the back seat.

A creeping fear overcame us. The future was an unlit pathway through a dark wood. If it took a roomful of experts to diagnose autism, how could we possibly cope with raising a child with this condition? Who would love and care for him when we were no longer there? We studied websites, scoured newspaper articles, sounded out friends whose friends had autistic children, and waded through piles of leaflets. Comfort was in short supply. At its worst it was blatant quackery, offering miracle cures in return for our life savings, the cost inflated by middle-class guilt: how will you live with yourself if you don't lay down everything you have to banish the demons of autism?

It took another eighteen months for Euan to be diagnosed. A team of specialists observed him for three days in a nursery environment, carrying out a series of structured assessments under the cover of playing with him in a clinical version of *The Truman Show*. The outcome was a three-page report culminating in a pithy last paragraph that defined Euan as having what was then called 'classic autism with learning difficulties'.

The news was handed down by two paediatricians sitting across a low circular table from us in a coldly lit clinical room. The autism diagnosis was a blow to the stomach, but at least we were ready for it. 'Learning difficulties', on the other hand, was a flying kick to the groin.

At home I sat on the staircase in the gloom of a January afternoon and cried silently. The diagnosis had been beyond our worst imaginings. There was light on the woodland pathway, but it brought no warmth.

Adam was born a few months before we knew about Euan's autism. As a toddler he made eye contact, answered people who talked to him and sat at the table mashing his food with his hands, just like any other two-year-old. But as the months went by, and the shock of Euan's diagnosis wore off, we began paying closer attention. We watched Adam sit in the middle of the floor beside a pile of toys, pick them up one by one, pass them closely in front of his eyes and put them down on the other side, working through the stack like an inspector on a production line. He would only eat if the food was served on a yellow plate. He ran up and down the garden path with his head to one side, captivated by the stroboscopic effect of the light between the fence slats.

More tellingly, his speech dried up at the age of two. Suddenly he would not utter a word to anybody other than his parents and his brother. Even well-known visitors such as his grandparents received only a hard, inquiring stare. 'Hello, Adam, are you talking today?' became my father's standard greeting, to my silent irritation.

I saw the dread creep across Magteld's face, and I can only assume she saw it on mine, too. Rather than marking the milestones of his development, like good competitive parents, we watched more and more for repetitive or unusual traits. We wondered if he might be mimicking his brother's behaviour. Perhaps he was even traumatised by it, though he and Euan clearly had a strong bond, so much so that it sometimes seemed as if Adam understood his brother better than we did.

For a time we had convinced ourselves we were raising one neurotypical child alongside an autistic one. It was a seductive idea: one brother would grow up with a 'normal life', study, get married, buy a house and have a career. In retrospect it was deeply unfair on both boys to see one as the salvation of the other.

At least the path to diagnosis was more straightforward this time. We knew who to call and what to expect, and our experience deterred the experts from dismissing us as over-anxious parents. Adam was diagnosed with autism at the age of three. With support, they said, he would be able to follow a regular school curriculum. But once again we had to reset the course of our family life.

What makes a successful marriage? It's one of the few questions, along with the one about the secret of a long and healthy life, that we look to the elderly to answer. But longevity is a poor way to measure success. Supportive, enriching marriages can shrivel and burn out within a decade, while other partnerships shiver on for decades after the fire has gone out.

The boys' diagnosis exposed the cracks in our relationship. Exactly when this happened is a fuzzy spot in my memory. I remember being on holiday in Bavaria's Urdonautal, a former basin of the Danube that had been abandoned by the river, leaving a shallow flat-bottomed valley peppered with statues of the Virgin, and being convinced that it was the last fortnight we would spend abroad as a family. But when we got home my resolve faltered.

And so we carried on, as unhappy couples do, stamping our feet as we sank into the quicksand. I even made a brief foray into stand-up comedy, but quickly realised that whatever state our marriage was in, telling cumbersome jokes to drunken students was no way to end or fix it. Magteld never directly reproached me, because we had passed the point where we could talk honestly, but once, after one of my less successful outings, she gave me a venomous look as she was carrying a basket of washing up the stairs and said, 'I told you it was shite.' After half a dozen trial runs, which at least yielded an article for the magazine where I was working and a cheque for £10, I hung up the pinstriped suit for good.

The end of a relationship is rarely a clean break and usually a messy unravelling: a slow aggregation of petty differences, jealousies, regrets, diverging ambitions and acts of dishonesty, great and small. After Adam was diagnosed Magteld sought treatment for depression, and I felt lost and powerless: too weak to lift her up, too dispirited to escape being dragged down.

We separated for a week. It began when I sat across the kitchen table opposite Magteld one morning, as muted autumn sunlight streamed into the room, and told her, 'I don't think we should be together any more.'

She looked more resigned than surprised. Deep down I think she had been expecting this moment, but she lived as if she could put it off for ever, like death. We took a walk around the block, trudging through the carpet of yellowing leaves on the pavement. I felt regret but also relief. Though our love was exhausted, I still felt affection for her. And we needed to do the best thing for the boys.

Later in the kitchen she said, 'I really looked up to you, you know.' It was a shock, both the choice of words and the past tense, the way she meekly accepted the blow. She would go back to Holland with the boys, she said, while I sorted myself out. She phoned her mother, who promised to get her old bedroom ready, perhaps a little too enthusiastically.

'*Ik vind het stiekem wel gezellig,*' Diny added, meaning: I secretly think it's quite nice.

I worked out how much money I would need to fly over every two weeks, and how I could meet the cost. I had started a new job not long before that involved working evenings and weekends and which, as my boss perceptively noted, was 'best suited to people who are divorced'. In the long term I thought I could move to the Netherlands independently. We could be a model divorced couple, devoted both to the children and to our own, separate, happiness.

Magteld took a different view. Moving back into the bedroom she had left as a teenager was not the way she planned to return. The last thing she wanted was to be judged for flying away in pursuit of a dream only to return with her wings scorched by a failed relationship. Nor did she relish the prospect of raising two demanding children on her own by working in a provincial flower shop. She feared the humiliating glances, misplaced sympathy and intrusive acts of kindness from people who had never been troubled by ambition.

That we didn't split was entirely down to Magteld's resourcefulness and quiet determination. I was spent, ready to quit our fraying marriage to chase a mirage. She took the threads and bound them together. Her initial reply, 'I really looked up to you', was a stroke of genius. It sowed the first real doubt in my mind. Was our relationship really so desolate if she could still assert that? Why did I think I would be any happier outside it?

First she coaxed me back into bed from the spare room.

And then, at her instigation, we began to talk. It quickly became apparent that what was missing was the verbal connection. Once we started communicating, the future came back into focus. The misty ambitions that had floated around our minds for years were welded into hard plans. We would move to Holland together, as a family. We set a deadline to leave by Euan's tenth birthday, just over two years away. In the meantime I would start looking for work while Magteld would look up schools. We decided we would live in The Hague, near her sister, Sanneke, with good work prospects and only twelve hours away from my parents by sea.

It's impossible to be dispassionate about the near-breakdown of your own marriage. The urge to revise history is irresistible. Many of the wounds in divorce are inflicted in the aftermath, when the differences between the two sides have become political. Similarly, when relationships survive we tend to ignore the fault lines that are always just below the surface, threatening to tear them apart. Love, left untended, will wither. What survived in our case, is the core truth: a year before Magteld was diagnosed with cancer, I told her I wasn't in love with her any more. And she refused to accept it.

I sometimes look back to those days and wonder how events would have played out if we had stayed apart. Would she have found a new partner who loved, cherished and supported her? How would I have felt, then, about being a bit player in her last act? Would I have felt jealous or inadequate about not being required when she was most in need, or grateful to have passed on the responsibility? Would we have reconciled and begun to forge a new relationship only for cancer to crush those fragile hopes too? What if she chose to face it alone, either fearfully aloof or sustained by the warmth of true friendship? Could I have stood by and watched as her strength faded and her body crumpled? Would there still have been time to laugh, to kiss, to embrace, to wipe the tears from her cheeks? What is certain is that guilt, anguish and regret would have been unavoidable, regardless of what choice I made. I know that because I have those feelings now.

*

Everyone with an autistic child knows this story. You're queuing at the supermarket checkout or waiting to be served in a restaurant or on a packed train, and your son or daughter is being driven to distraction by the noise, by the cacophony of faces, by the rattle of the carriages or the passing crockery or the squeaking trolley wheels. They pull you by the arm, scream, run up and down, screw up their faces in confusion and alarm. People start to stare and nudge each other until someone says, just loud enough for you to hear, 'Parents these days have no control,' eliciting a round of quiet nods.

Autism is sometimes defined as absence of empathy. What, then, is the excuse of the stranger who denounces you in the supermarket without consideration? One thing autism has taught me is that almost everyone overestimates their capacity for empathy. Paradoxically, it's a self-serving concept: we tend to ascribe good motives to ourselves and malign ones to others, on a sliding scale. Those closest to us are more likely to be seen as trustworthy, while those who are different or unfamiliar are instinctively treated with suspicion.

Appealing to prejudice is the foundation stone of every good con trick. Consider the last time you were off sick from work. You sat at home, worried about the workload piling up in your absence, regretting the missed appointments and feeling guilty towards the colleagues who filled in for you.

Because of that you probably went back too early. Yet when someone else is absent from the office you're more likely to wonder if they're really that ill, and if another colleague disparages them you'll feel your suspicions were justified. Empathy is hard work; it requires conscious, deliberate thought and a measure of self-denial. We are easily seduced by any argument that lets us off the hook. No gossip is more gleefully shared than the news that the victim of a terrible plight has brought it on themselves, because mockery is light relief while empathy is burdensome.

Autism has taught me that empathy has two stages: understanding and communication. Autistic people struggle with the second of these; everyone else – neurotypicals – tends to skim the first, preferring to 'pick up signals' and read 'body language' rather than scrutinise someone else's feelings. The sick worker's absence gives rise to gossip among his colleagues, which rapidly develops into a coherent narrative. Rumours, especially vicious ones, have a mimetic quality: the more they are repeated, the more freely and boldly they are expressed, the more credible they seem. Suspicion spreads like a virus, branding the waylaid colleague a notorious shirker.

This is the phenomenon known as groupthink. And autistic people don't, in my experience, do groupthink. To me it's one of their most distinguishing features. They don't fall in with the collective lies and bogus virtues that can mislead a crowd. They are oblivious to the distorting prism of received opinion.

When I remember how much empathy Euan and Adam displayed towards their sick mother, I find it impossible to accept the idea that it is incompatible with autism. They winced visibly when she descended into her coughing fits, moved into her bed to comfort her at night and protected her fiercely when exhaustion or anxiety overwhelmed her. When we went to the supermarket Euan told me to buy medicine for his mother because she wasn't well; another time he instructed me to read his bedtime story because 'Mum's tired'. For a boy so attached to a set daily routine, these small concessions required a huge adjustment to the order of the universe. 'They may not know it, but their biggest superpower is them being themselves,' Magteld wrote. 'They play a big part in getting me through it.'

Autism didn't destroy our marriage, but it revealed the neglected corners, the cracks in the foundations and the crumbling walls. It was also our first encounter with grief.

At first sight it may seem perverse to grieve for a child who is alive and healthy. But, as Jim Sinclair observed in his essay 'Don't Mourn For Us', grief is a common reaction among parents whose children are diagnosed with autism. Working through it is part of the process of acceptance, which is why many quack therapists depend on locking parents into the grief cycle in order to persuade them that their worthless treatments will restore a child who never truly existed.

Sinclair contended that parents of autistic children grieve not for the child they have but the one they wanted. 'It isn't about autism, it's about shattered expectations,' he wrote. The inquisitive toddler, the sociable ten-year-old, the precocious teenager, the student turning up every third weekend with a sackload of washing, the young man or woman striking out on the path of job, home, car, partner. Much family tension has its origins in those moments when children deviate from this prescribed route, but for most parents the adjustments are small and gradual. Autism, by contrast, arrives early on like a ten-ton weight dropping from a clear blue sky.

At first I scolded myself for grieving. Why were we mourning a child who needed our unconditional love and attention? But all this did was trigger feelings of guilt, which compounded the grief. We had to abandon our aspirations and learn to accept Euan and Adam for themselves. It taught me a lesson I would rely on later: that grief is a healing process, a way of coming to terms with catastrophic changes that are beyond your control. Without grief we have only anger, hopelessness and despair. Grief hurts, but refusing to grieve does even worse damage.

It took time to acquire the patience our children needed. It started by acknowledging that the burden fell on them, not us, and our job was to guide them. Not to scorn or shun or straighten or 'cure' them, teach them to mask their autism or try to fit them into a different mould. They needed to be nurtured, not exorcised. However hard it felt for us, and it was sometimes grindingly hard, we constantly reminded ourselves that if we faltered, they would fall. And this was the second lesson I learned: nobody has to suffer from autism, but without the right support, autistic people can, and do, suffer terribly.

When Magteld was diagnosed with cancer, Miss Winter had warned her to be alert for peddlers of bogus cures. Magteld laughed for the first time that day and reassured the surgeon that autism had immunised her against quackery. Cancer shamans employ the same false certainties, duplicitous language and fear dressed up as hope, the same grief-farming chicanery. We understood from the start that her treatment was going to be long, painful and exhausting. We knew there would be no miracle cures; we had to embrace uncertainty. All Magteld could do was keep taking the pills and live every day as if it wasn't her last.

*

Yes, there were times when it all got too much: the treadmill of treatment and sickness, the aching exhaustion, the asphyxiating fear. A high concentration of these elements would precipitate a tempestuous row. Sometimes I fled through the front door, leaving Magteld alone with her rage while I ploughed ahead blindly, not stopping until all the fury and shame and impotence had been trampled into the paving stones. It was never the respectful or the reasonable thing to do, but sometimes it felt like the only option. Then I would come to rest on a bench and await the phone call that would begin the long, chastening process of reconciliation.

The lowest point came on a Monday morning in early December. Rain had been teeming from a pewter sky for what seemed like months. The boys were in a slow frenzy, jumping up and down the stairs and erupting in geyser-like rage. The night beforehand, Magteld and I had watched an episode of *The Killing* in which one of the background characters was a young mother who died of cancer. I hadn't even noticed it, but Magteld's radar was more finely attuned. We slept intermittently, swathed in fear. As she stirred the porridge pot at breakfast, she boiled with anxiety. What if the treatment failed, what were the chances of the cancer returning, what if it surfaced in another part of her body?

I had no answers. I couldn't soothe her pain. I wished I had a bouquet of hope, sweet and gleaming, that I could hold under her nose. I wanted to tell her it would work out, she would recover, we would conquer cancer together and emerge, swords aloft and smiling. But it was a brittle and worthless fantasy that crumbled in the hard light of fate.

Magteld was standing over the cooker, her back turned to me and shaking. She was sobbing noiselessly. I was by the table next to the door, in the opposite corner of the dining kitchen, itching to flee. On the corner of the table was a small glass. As I left the room I picked it up and weighed it for a second, feeling the smooth hard material in my trembling hand.

I launched the glass full-tilt into the wall. It seemed to

shatter even before it left my hand. I heard the smash a fraction of a second later, like the blast of a gun, but didn't look back.

Magteld wailed after me as I retreated up the stairs. At first she thought I had knocked something onto the floor. Only when she turned around did she see the blasted fragments spreading out from the wall, across the floor and over the table.

Sweeping up the glass later, I wondered how these memories would affect us as survivors. Once the treatment was over, once Magteld's hair had grown back, exhaustion had been banished, fear had been neutered and the whole macabre opera had been played out – once, in short, we emerged from our year in hell – what would be left of us? I was becoming a caricature, an impotent manchild venting his frustration on the tableware. My sick wife needed comfort and I gave her glass splinters, across the floor, embedded in the picture rail, in the fruit bowl.

Would the cracks and blisters heal over, or would they linger beneath the surface, ready to burst open at the next onslaught?

How much of the debris of these days would cling to us?

I fetched the stepladder and switched two pictures on the wall to cover the damaged plasterwork. We slept a little better that night.

6

The mood had lightened, mercifully, by the time Magteld's birthday came around, on 5 March. The first buds were pushing through on the trees and she felt her old energy returning as the days grew warmer and brighter, allowing her to take more frequent and longer walks. Sometimes she went on her own; sometimes we went together. Her hair was growing back, a darker colour than her former wheat-blonde and thicker in texture. Mainly we were relieved to have got past the winter and the operation. Those fraught days when she was flitting in and out of hospital were already fading from memory and for the first time since her chemotherapy began, our lives had a sense of rhythm.

In the summer we would go on holiday to Denmark with her sister's family, take the children to Legoland and put the house up for sale. But before that there was radiotherapy. If chemotherapy was carpet bombing and the mastectomy a targeted strike, radiotherapy was the scorched-earth campaign to choke the cancer at the root. Magteld would have twenty ten-minute sessions, once a day, five days a week, lying prone on a bed while radiation beams were blasted into the crater that the tumour had left behind.

She insisted on travelling alone to the clinic, even though it involved a ten-minute walk to the railway station, a change of trains at Glasgow Central and another ten-minute walk up to the Beatson Cancer Centre. Glasgow's weather can be mischievous in April, stirring up horizontal rain and face-whipping winds even on a bright day, but it was commendably restrained for the month of her treatment. On one of the first days she phoned me to say she had fainted at the station and been sick on the platform. She was still fragile and, having lost so much weight after the operation, prone to dizziness. Before I could think of riding to her rescue, she had boarded the next train and carried on. She refused to give up her solo journey, but from then on she packed a banana in her handbag.

After each session she dropped in at the Maggie's Centre next to the hospital, to drink coffee and chat with the volunteers and fellow cancer patients. The building was on a hill overlooking the Beatson, designed by the Dutch architect Rem Koolhaas to capture as much light as possible. There were formal events, workshops and counselling sessions, but also the chance to sit and talk, or just sit. It was a place that ran on mutual respect and dignity, where cancer patients could shield themselves from the pressure to fight, or be brave, or inspire people healthier than themselves.

Sometimes the only people she could relate to were those who were going through the same process, who didn't judge or flinch from discussing the worst aspects. New visitors were often surprised to find that the atmosphere was convivial and optimistic. When Magteld went back to the Beatson the following year, this time as a patient who would not recover, she drew again on the deep resources of compassion and understanding at Maggie's.

*

Magteld was afflicted with a terrible sense of direction. On an early visit to Edinburgh she went for a walk in the city centre and wandered out towards Haymarket, where she called me from a payphone. She laughed about it then, but it was an early indication of the fear of disorientation that haunted her through her life. For a long time I failed to realise how inhibiting it was to be unable to read the contours of a city or translate the lines of a map into an orderly route. It was a kind of blindness, more profound than being unable to tell left from right, which she also struggled with. Eventually salvation arrived in the form of satellite navigation technology.

Having failed three driving tests in the Netherlands, it took her five years to get behind the wheel again, but in Northampton she passed first time, in defiance of the town's deranged traffic planning. Another five would go by before she overcame her phobia of going out in the car alone. It happened quite suddenly. I had the job of collecting Euan from nursery, which meant catching a train home from work, picking up the car and driving out to fetch him. I was full of resentment, not understanding why Magteld should be so terrified of losing her way on a journey of less than a mile. And then one afternoon I came home to find Euan sitting at the kitchen table, laughing gleefully, and Magteld beside him, beaming in triumph, as if she had butchered a dragon for supper.

Another time she took Euan to the doctor's surgery, which was fifteen minutes away along a well-known route. An hour later she phoned, her voice crackling with despair, from Anniesland Cross, five miles adrift and on the opposite bank of the River Clyde. How on earth, I thought scornfully, could you not notice you were crossing the river? Euan was burbling in the background, oblivious to his mother's anguish. Eventually she persuaded a taxi driver to escort her back across the river to her own neighbourhood. He had the compassion and sensitivity not to charge her. A passing cabbie saw in an instant what I had dismissively overlooked for years: that Magteld was ashamed and distressed at being unable to find her way.

The upside to Magteld's wayward sense of direction was that it turned every journey into an adventure.

On one of the first evenings I spent with her in Sleen we went to the cashpoint. Soft rain flickered in the streetlights as we crossed the wet streets to the bank, on the other side of the village. On the way home I noticed we were going a different way. 'Is this the scenic route?' I asked, at which she laughed nervously. We clasped hands and meandered slowly back to the house. She smiled with relief as we approached the front door, where I brushed her wet hair from her face and kissed her.

'The scenic route' became a recurring motif whenever one of us took a little too long to come back from the supermarket.

It didn't stop her enjoying hillwalking, and sometimes enhanced the experience. On a weekend in Glen Coe we set out from the village on a bright May morning to conquer Bidean nam Bian, one of the peaks looming over the village. Surely, we thought, it would be a simple matter, once at the summit, to walk along the ridge and back down again, guiding ourselves by the main road. But once on the ridge we lost sight of the road and trudged through the band of snow capping the summit, bagging another peak and making our way down a matted hillside where the thick grass was undisturbed by walkers' boots. As we picked our way down and the sun fell behind the hill we started to worry where the road had gone. It had been some time since we had seen another walker. Weariness was starting to creep in. And then we saw, further up the hillside, a brown speck, and another, and as we looked more closely we realised a herd of deer was traversing the hill. They moved majestically, loose-limbed and unruffled, unlike the coy specimens that quiver by the roadside. We sat, silent and awestruck, for a few minutes, before continuing down the mountain.

Half an hour later, as a gloom spread through the valley, we made out the dark contour of the road and tramped towards it, where the driver of a passing campervan stopped and took us to the village. It was a good two miles away, and we were relieved not to have had to cover it on foot.

Magteld measured the progress of her cancer treatment in the same terms: not as a conventional straight line or charted territory that could be expressed in trig points and contours, but as a forest trail of makeshift paths and sudden clearings. In her first blog after being diagnosed she wrote: 'I'm not always going to be brave and the road will be a bit rocky at times, but I'll have the odd route touristique too.' All our journeys have the same destination; all that differs is how we get there.

*

I wanted to fall in love with Magteld again. Properly, this time.

Once we had accepted the children's autism, once we had resolved to stop grieving and stay together, from this day forward, in sickness and in health, we could start making up for lost time. We had moved between cities and across borders, laughed and danced and cried and fought and made love. Like long-discarded cocoons, the two self-absorbed teenagers who had met in Italy bore no resemblance to the people we were now. Magteld had acquired a capacity for exhaustive negotiation, the kind that had allowed the Dutch to tame their landscape and shape their country over centuries, and discovered untapped reserves of guile and tenacity.

She gave up work soon after Adam was diagnosed so she could pour all her energy into the boys' care. Special-needs education required her to learn a new vocabulary and feed the insatiable bureaucratic Minotaur. She needed the skill and patience of a watchmaker to make sure the cogs of the system kept turning in harmony. Her diary filled up with meetings where she juggled educational psychologists, speech and language therapists, social workers, occupational therapists, school teachers, nursery staff, play workers and child psychiatrists. She became adept at nudging and coercing officials to see things her way. Calm, assured, decisive, nerveless and sometimes as stubborn as a rusty doornail.

Euan's diagnosis came too late for him to be placed in special education, so he spent his first year in the local primary school. The school was in a draughty building at the top of a hill, and as autumn tightened its grip the wind and rain swirled around the roof, howling and battering like a starving wolf. Euan became too agitated to stay in the group, and his classroom assistant took him out for walks around the playground. After a year he transferred to another school, three miles away, that was better suited to his needs.

When Adam's turn came he was offered, after months of prevarication, a place in a different school that catered for children with challenging behaviour. Magteld drove out to see it and concluded quickly that it would be a disastrous move for a boy who hardly spoke and was highly sensitive to noise and tension. She called a meeting that afternoon with the deputy head of Euan's former school, and by the end of the day had secured him a place. The council officials tried everything to coax and cajole her into changing her mind, but Magteld had learned to say no with a smile.

When Euan's school needed a new chair for the parent council her name was put forward and, somewhat to her own surprise, she accepted. She went on to become an advocate for carers, making some of her closest friends in the world of grassroots campaigning and going on lobbying forays to the Scottish Parliament. As more people exploited her aptitude for diplomacy she had to concede that she possessed it. Euan's school had struggled for years with a leaking roof; half-full buckets were a standard feature in the classrooms and grew in number through the winter. Plans for a new roof had been stalled for years because the council balked at the cost. Magteld harnessed the resources of the parent council to support the school in a fresh campaign. By compiling a log of all the patchwork repairs carried out over the years, the parent council showed that over time they cost just as much money as a new roof, and the children were still having their lessons in leaking classrooms. By the time Magteld stood down as chair two years later, following her diagnosis, the funding had been secured.

Anxiety could still seize her on the cusp of an important meeting. She could reduce herself to a wreck envisaging catastrophic scenarios in which she committed a fatal error or was upbraided by a forceful speaker. But when she began talking, people couldn't help but listen. She had a gift for taming an audience, perhaps because she connected with and shared their worries. Time and again she entered a room under a cloud and emerged bathed in sunlight.

She took huge satisfaction from outwitting experienced professionals. Learning to raise two autistic children had been daunting at first, but it unlocked Magteld's finest qualities and introduced her to people whose company she valued: passionate and caring, sometimes idealistic, tenacious and uncompromising, refusing to bow to fate. The name Magteld, or Mechtild, or Matilda, means strength in battle. Fifteen years earlier I had fallen in love with a slip of a girl with an awkward smile and gazelle-like legs. The second time it was with the warrior.

*

We celebrated the conclusion of her radiotherapy with lunch in a brasserie near the hospital, five minutes' walk from our old flat on the Great Western Road. In some ways it was a revival of the celebrations that had been suspended when cancer scuppered my birthday eight months earlier. Time could begin again. We ate pasta, drank orange juice and toasted the future. It was a vivid blue Friday morning in April, and we were starting to look ahead once more.

Magteld had expected to feel unburdened. For four weeks she had made the pilgrimage to the Beatson, taking two trains and walking up the hill to be peppered with invisible grapeshot. A square burn mark had formed beneath her shoulder, and in the last few days it had started to blister and weep. She had been warned to keep out of the summer sun in case the treatment had damaged her skin's resistance.

In the beginning Magteld set her teeth against anything that defined her as a cancer patient, but as the months went by it became part of her identity. Getting through the treatment dominated her field of vision so strongly that it obscured the usual concerns about the future. Now that the veil was lifted, she felt suddenly vulnerable, as if she had stepped naked out of a dark forest. What was she supposed to do now? 'I felt anxious, as if I had lost something,' she wrote. 'Suddenly I lost my focus. I had spent the best part of a year being treated for cancer. I was constantly preparing myself for the next treatment.'

After eight months she had to stumble back into the outside world. She had plans: a visit to her family in June, the holiday in Denmark in August. Above all we wanted to get on with moving to the Netherlands after our year in hell. But these aspirations, which had sustained us through the tough months, now had to be given substance. As emigration became a serious prospect, the attendant challenges shifted into focus.

By the time we visited her family in June, Magteld's hair had grown back to a short copper-beech coating. A heatwave had set in, with temperatures spiking at thirty-five degrees. On a visit to the *hunebedden* a few miles up the road, the boys leapt between the monolithic tombstones, monuments to a forgotten people, as she looked on. Six weeks had passed since her treatment and she was already acquiring a glow.

We planned to put the house up for sale in August. It belonged to a different era now: before autism, before cancer, before the near-collapse of our marriage. The estate agent, a puffy-cheeked, fussily polite man in his fifties, assured us we would have no trouble selling the house but advised us not to rush into a sale.

We flew to Copenhagen, drove for three hours across Denmark and arrived late in the evening. The boys were tired, but the prospect of a night in a pirate-themed hotel room was fixed in their minds like the north star. Three days in the park were designed to dispel the memories of the harrowing months behind us and restore the cycle of our days and weeks. We flew back to Glasgow as the sun was setting, heading due west so that the lingering daylight was frozen in a reddish glow. A sense of suppressed elation flowed through us. After we had spent so long in limbo the hope was powerful enough to burn us.

Before we left Scotland we wanted to take the children for a walk in the hills. Opportunities for climbing would be in short supply in the Netherlands. So on a Saturday morning in early September we packed a picnic bag, pulled on our hiking boots and set off for Tinto Hill, a steady climb to over 2,300 feet and the highest peak in the Southern Uplands, with views from the summit to England.

We parked the car and set off up the slope. The narrow gravel path unwound beyond us like a ribbon. The boys skipped on ahead, revelling in the open space, and we asked ourselves why we hadn't taken them walking more often. Now that our time in Scotland's unkempt terrain was nearing its end we wanted to become better acquainted with it.

We ate sandwiches by a giant flat-sided boulder, took some photographs and carried on up as the path became steeper and narrower. The wind, which was a gentle current at the base of the hill, gathered in strength, ruffling our collars and teasing our hair and faces.

Eventually we came to a junction. To the right was a straight, steady rise to the summit; to the left, a trail across a small plateau ended in a cairn. Magteld had begun to struggle in the last few hundred metres and wanted to turn back. She had underestimated how long it would take to recover from her treatment. My instinct was to head for the summit with the boys, staying true to our original aim. She shook her head and told me sternly that none of us was going any further. This was the turning point. We would walk to the cairn and go back down, as a family.

We picked our way across the bog and looked down at the grey ribbon that led back to Glasgow. It was a good way down; we were closer to the summit than the base. We held hands and stood silently as the coarse grass rippled around our ankles. It was time to go home, we told the boys. They cheered and scrambled back down the hill, followed by me, supporting a weary Magteld. I felt a niggle of regret at missing the summit, but I was glad we had at least tried.

Magteld would have to take tamoxifen for the next five years. It was not so much a prescription as a sentence. Every morning she woke up, cancer was sitting up by her bedside, demanding attention. Before getting out of bed, she squeezed two pills from a blister pack and swallowed them with water.

Within a few weeks she was squirming in bed, racked by hot flushes. She complained of cold, tiredness and sore knees. Her periods stopped. The drug that was guarding her against the recurrence of her disease had also triggered the onset of the menopause. It fended off death with one hand and dismissed youth with the other. Her memory wavered occasionally – only for an instant, but long enough to make her feel vulnerable. She lacked the energy to take up running, so she began swimming in the mornings, among the sprightlier pensioners. Old age had swept in, like a mugger in an alleyway, leaving her breathless and frightened.

Magteld went on television to speak about the high proportion of women who abandon tamoxifen. Why, she was asked, would they refuse to take a drug that was keeping them alive? It was the lack of preparation, she said. Patients were essentially given a prescription, instructed to take the pills and left to discover the downsides for themselves. Some found the consequences – broken nights, depression and weight gain – more onerous than the cancer treatment itself. And there was no guarantee that the disease would not return. But it gave Magteld hope, and despite the side effects she continued to take it.

It's easily forgotten that medicine is essentially poison. Benign poison, but doctors put too much faith in reason's ability to overcome this basic fear. Every cancer patient knows the percentage game and adopts their own strategy. Empathy, with its capacity to understand fear and pain, is a more effective communication tool than plain directives to do the sensible thing.

Magteld was due to see Miss Winter on Hallowe'en for her first six-monthly check-up. It was the last hurdle in our way. If she passed we could focus all our efforts on emigrating.

At the end of September we visited Sanneke in The Hague for Adam's eighth birthday. At this stage our knowledge of the city was limited to the central station, Sanneke's house and a few streets in between. A bus took us on a meandering route from our rented flat in Scheveningen through the suburbs. We looked out of the window at rows of shops, monumental redbrick churches and neatly paved streets, trying to imagine where we might live.

We took the liberty of viewing an apartment, even though our house in Glasgow was resolutely unsold. It was a curious construction, with a large living room on the ground floor, a small kitchen at the back and a corridor leading through to four bedrooms piled one on top of the other up a fearsomely narrow staircase. A hammock was slung across the patio doors at the back and immediately invoked dreams of summer afternoons spent idling in the sun, dozing off with a book in hand. The facade resembled a bell tower, a fussy arrangement of red and white bricks with two recessed balconies, crowned by a narrow turret. The three upstairs rooms had fallen into disuse because the elderly couple who lived there could no longer climb the staircase. The estate agent told us they had been waiting to move for three years. How disquieting, I thought, to be cut off from parts of your own house.

As we walked round with the agent we explained that we

were moving from Scotland. Towards the end of the tour he said in a lowered tone, '*In de afgelopen tijd is dit land wat minder geworden.*' This country isn't what it used to be. I had got used to hearing Dutch people say this for years – particularly abroad, and usually with a pinch of humblebrag: 'It's the country that got small, not me'. But this felt like I was being entrusted with a vital secret. It was certainly a striking confession from someone who was trying to persuade us to buy a house there.

From there we took the ten-minute tram journey to the beach. What bliss, we said to each other, to have the sea so close at hand. We sat outside a beach hut in oversized wooden chairs and basked in the September sunshine as the children ran down to the shore and jumped in the waves. 'It's not normally like this,' Sanneke warned us. All the more reason to savour it, I thought, as I took off my shoes and sank my feet into the warm sand.

Next year, we thought. Next year we will be here again, definitely.

The nights closed in. Our house refused to sell, and it became clear we wouldn't be moving before Christmas.

The waiting was like plodding through a swamp in the fog. The boys depended on us to untangle the future, but we were at the mercy of one of the most irrational forces in the world: the whims of house hunters. It was too small, or had too many rooms, or was too bruised from the impact of two boisterous children. One fastidious couple condemned it on the basis of a leaky gutter. We tried to bear it bravely. After stalling for a year Magteld was impatient to rebuild her life in her own country, and we were both becoming restless.

As the flow of viewers slowed to a trickle, our sense of stagnation deepened. Magteld started to worry she would be stuck in the house. Our former neighbours on the corner, two doors away and with a more spacious garden, had taken more than a year to sell theirs. The boys were also starting to feel the strain. Adam wanted to know if he would miss his sports day, while Euan simply asked over and over again when we would be living in Holland. Easter, we said, more in hope than expectation.

In the weeks before she saw Miss Winter, Magteld consulted other cancer patients on how to deal with this new and ambiguous fixture in her life. There was no such thing as the 'all-clear'. The disease was never banished. The best outcome was to be told that it was dormant and she could reasonably expect to live another six months. It was like a drawn-out game of Russian roulette, because if the cancer showed up in another part of her body there was no going back.

Miss Winter told her there were no signs of the cancer returning and scheduled the next appointment for the end of April. We arranged to spend Christmas in Norwich with my parents. The house-hunting season was winding down and our best hope now was that a buyer would materialise early in the New Year.

On 9 November Magteld had a farewell lunch with her friends from the local carers' group. Many of them had been with us at the picnic in Paisley, just over a year earlier, when she was still reeling from her diagnosis. Now she could celebrate with them, raise a glass of prosecco and look forward to life in The Hague. They gave her a silver heart and a scarf: the former as a souvenir of their friendship, the latter to wrap around herself whenever she was feeling low or in need of a hug. She looked happy and bright, they said, and excited about the future.

Around the same time she developed a niggling cough. It was early November, the time of year when colds go on the rampage in Glasgow's dank climate. Ordinarily there would have been no reason to give it a second thought, but Magteld knew that every blip in her health from now on came with unwelcome insinuations. A cough was never just a cough.

It was nothing to worry about, she told her friends. She'd just had her six-month check-up.

Early in December she visited the chemotherapy ward, brandishing a card and a box of chocolates, her hair and vitality restored. The nurses recognised her instantly. For a quarter of an hour she basked in the warmth and compassion that had carried her through those terrible months a year earlier.

She talked animatedly, smiling all the while, interrupted occasionally by her persistent cough.

She went swimming once a week, on Tuesday mornings, among the pensioners who glided unhurriedly up and down the lanes. It was getting harder for her to keep up with them, and she emerged from the pool panting with the effort.

You should see the doctor, I implored her, but she resisted with gritted teeth. She wasn't blind to the dangers; she was too sharply aware of them. She wanted to enjoy Christmas with her boys, and no cough was going to deny her. If it was still there in January she would see the doctor then. She clenched her jaw and lowered her eyes. If the worst news was around the corner, it could wait a little longer.

On the day she visited the hospital the last leaves of the season were tumbling from the tops of the trees, just as they had done a year earlier when she looked out of the window from the blue chair, her head bare, her arm tied to a drip feed.

The new year's foliage would outlive her.

It was a Friday night, late in November, crisp and black, and I was sitting at my desk with my jacket on, all set to pack up for the night. I was working two evenings a week on Scottish Television's news website, earning just enough to keep a stricken family going. I thought of Magteld, how she was probably curled up under the bedsheets already, and the way she opened her eyes and smiled when I came home just before midnight and slipped in beside her, feeling her soft warmth and clasping her delicate hand.

On a regular Friday evening no more than five people were in the newsroom. Just as I was about to leave, a colleague came over and alerted me to a tweet from Jim Murphy, the Labour MP for Eastwood. He wrote: 'Awful scenes in Glasgow. Helicopter crashed into a pub.'

There wasn't much else. The photograph Murphy had

taken showed a jagged black mass squatting on top of a flat-roofed building. The pub was recognisable as the Clutha Vaults, a live-music venue whose Friday-evening gigs had a strong following. It was about ten minutes' walk from the office, and already the wail of ambulance sirens swirled in the night air. I sent my colleague down to find out more, put one hand on the phone and started scrolling through internet channels with the other.

By the time my colleague arrived on the scene it was clear we were dealing with a terrible disaster. The police helicopter had ploughed vertically through the roof of the pub. A newspaper editor, getting into his car at the top of a multi-storey car park, watched it drop noiselessly out of the sky like a dying bird. Inside, around 120 people were sitting drinking and enjoying a gig by a local ska band. They had set out from all parts of the city in the darkness, brought together by the lure of a few hours' music and revelry. None of them had doubted they would see daylight again.

Colleagues began drifting into the office. Others surfaced online and snapped into working mode from wherever their Friday-night meanderings had dropped them: pubs, restaurants, taxi queues. Out of the chaos of facts a news story took form. Very quickly it became clear that at least six people had died, a number that climbed to nine during the night and reached its final total two weeks later when the tenth victim died in hospital.

At some point in the first hour I phoned Magteld. I wouldn't be coming home, I told her. 'I didn't think you would be,' she said. She had been watching the coverage on the television. I spent the next eight hours grinding out updates to the website. By the time I left the office at seven in the morning a bleary November sun was glowing on the horizon and ambulances were still screaming past as they conveyed the last casualties from the accident scene, a few hundred yards up the road.

Magteld's rasping cough embedded itself like a stubborn splinter. Sometimes it subsided for an hour or two and she would declare, 'My cough has gone!' But the respite was always too brief. It was just a wretched winter cold, she said, and once it was gone she could look forward again.

By Christmas she was starting to retch up specks of blood in the bathroom. Once again I implored her to see the doctor. No, she said, it was just the damp Glasgow air, the draughts in my parents' house, the stress of selling the house. How could she be so obdurate about her own health, I wondered in frustration. But her eyes betrayed the black moths fluttering in her head.

In the week after Christmas the estate agent called with more viewings. Two couples wanted to see the house on Hogmanay. We packed our bags and took the train north, sensing a change in fortunes was imminent. Her parents booked a ferry crossing to Newcastle in March, so they could help us prepare for the move.

Neither of the couples who came to the house had children, so it seemed unlikely they would take on a four-bedroom home, but we took it as an encouraging sign. On Hogmanay Magteld was too tired to stay up for the bells, so I went out into the garden alone, sat in the cold drizzle and saluted the New Year with a solitary whisky. Whatever awaited us in 2014, it couldn't possibly be more horrific than the year we'd just dispatched.

7

For most of history, death has been woven into the fabric of everyday life, but in these more mollycoddled times I didn't encounter it close-up until the age of thirty-three. In the last week of 2007, as the festive lights were fading in the winter gloom, my father and I caught a train to see Motherwell vs Dundee United. We weren't regular football-goers, but taking in a match had become a Christmas tradition. Magteld stayed at home with the boys and my mother, eating homemade cake.

We took our seats about six rows back from the touchline, sheltering unsuccessfully from the intermittent rain and cold. It was a graceless, shapeless, typically Scottish game, but with plenty of goals to keep the crowd warm. The standout moment was a sweeping move up the park by Motherwell that culminated in Stephen Hughes firing in a low drive from David Clarkson's lay-off. That made the score 1–0 and thereafter Motherwell took charge, scoring four more times, the best of the goals a floated chip by Clarkson, who was having a match to remember.

Twenty-two minutes had passed since Clarkson's second goal, and twelve more were left of a game that was fizzing out like a spent firework, when the home team won a corner. The ball drifted in a slow arc, gleaming in the floodlit night sky, towards the squirming figures in the penalty area. Then, quite inexplicably, one of them crumpled to the ground. Football fans are used to seeing players throw themselves to the ground theatrically, but this fall was different. Even at a distance of fifty yards in the gloom it disrupted the game like a hand grenade landing on a concert piano. The stadium instantly fell silent. The crowd of just over 5,000, which just minutes before had danced to the counterpoint of jovial hostility, was united in horror.

The player on the ground was Motherwell's captain, Phil O'Donnell. He was just about to be substituted: at the age of thirty-five, a veteran in footballing terms, he seemed to be tiring and had been outmanoeuvred for United's second goal, a few minutes earlier. He would take a handful more steps and feel his heart beat less than a thousand more times before he collapsed in the penalty area.

The spectators stood and applauded Phil O'Donnell as he departed the arena on a stretcher, still unmoving. The game, incongruously, resumed, but without the hostility it was a ghastly shadow theatre, and though Dundee United scored a third goal – the eighth altogether – nobody cheered, not even Noel Hunt, the scorer. The crowd drained away from the stadium, hushed and bemused. At eighteen minutes past five, as my father and I sat waiting for a train to take us home, Phil O'Donnell was pronounced dead in Wishaw General Hospital. His heart had stopped on the pitch, and the medical staff had been unable to revive him. His life had ended right there, in the white box of a playing field, among his fellow players, the match officials and 5,227 paying spectators.

The air felt numb as my father and I, along with a few dozen other match-goers, boarded the train back to Glasgow. At this point nobody knew for sure what had happened. A rumour went round the carriage that he had been revived in the club's medical room, but the collective sense in the stadium that something more serious was at hand was confirmed by my mother, who had been following the news on television and confirmed that of the twenty-two players who started the game at three o'clock, one had not survived the ninety minutes.

It seemed obscene that death could pluck out a fit young man in front of thousands of spectators in that modern celebration of youth and vitality, a sports match. David Clarkson must have been looking forward to celebrating his two goals later with Phil O'Donnell, who was not just his teammate and captain but also his uncle. Instead he was catapulted head first into the land of grief.

*

More house viewers came in the new year. The estate agent said it was encouraging: only the hardy and the desperate would look for a new home in Glasgow in the depth of winter. Magteld booked a flight to The Hague in February and lined up as many house viewings as she could manage. Her cough still plagued her, but she was determined to press ahead with our move to Holland. We scoured the online listings and hired a buying agent (the Dutch practice is to hire advisers on both sides, so that all the haggling and horse-trading is carried out in a safe environment by trained professionals). She also began looking into suitable schools. Adam would hopefully go to the local primary school with his cousins, but for Euan we faced a mountain of forms and assessments by a whole new posse of educational experts.

Halfway through January came the breakthrough. One of the viewers from Hogmanay came for a second viewing with his partner. By the end of the week we had agreed a price. I felt like a B-movie scientist who, after months working on a rattling contraption of pipes, dials and pistons, finally gets to pull the lever. I looked up removal companies and booked a ferry. We settled on a moving date of 25 April, a Friday, just after Easter, thirteen weeks away. Magteld embellished the entry in the diary with a smiley face.

The previous Thursday she had seen the doctor about her cough. It was probably just a winter cold, said the doctor, but given her history she booked an X-ray 'just to be sure'. The phrase made Magteld twitch with déjà vu. Her coughing was gradually getting worse and so was my creeping sense of dread. Some nights she sat up in bed, shaking and spluttering until her lungs were almost spent. Her eyes swam and her cheeks flushed with the effort of breathing. 'I'm OK, really,' she gasped.

We went to Edinburgh to try to settle our minds. After thirteen years in Scotland I felt like a tourist again. I had an ambition to see the castle one last time. Magteld toiled up the Royal Mile, and by the time we made it to the Esplanade, beneath an indigo sky, there were only fifteen minutes to go till closing time. A guard staunchly barred our way. 'Come back tomorrow,' she said.

I had an urge to charge past and growl something about not knowing if there'd be a tomorrow. Magteld looked at me, weary-faced, and said, 'Come on, let's go.' My cold anger drained away. We walked back down to a café just off the main road and warmed ourselves over hot chocolate and marshmallows. We focused on the positive things: the house was sold, Magteld was flying out to see Sanneke in a few weeks, and in three months' time we would be sailing to IJmuiden, with our lives boxed and packed into a removal van. It should have been fresh and inspiring. But every time her cough erupted I heard the hard clink of footsteps behind us.

The solicitors who handled our house sale worked out of a compact, bustling office in Giffnock, just outside Glasgow on the south side, loaded with papers and filing cabinets. Across a table was Nicky, the sales negotiator we had been in almost weekly contact with for four months without ever meeting. There was relief all round: for the lawyers, because the market was on the rise again after a long slump, and for us, because at last we could embark on our great adventure.

Magteld's cough had subsided and good-hearted chatter buzzed round the room as we skimmed the legal papers and signed our names at the bottom.

The next day we walked up to Adam's school in the afternoon, bouncing lightly and feeling bound together. I had to cut my pace up the shallow hill to accommodate Magteld, whose breathing was still a little laboured. Her news stirred a flurry of excitement among the other mothers in the playground. At home we drank coffee while Adam went out to his trampoline. It was a bright winter's day, and the future had suddenly opened, like a crocus in bud.

An uncorrected legacy of the previous owners of our house was that the main telephone was upstairs, in Adam's bedroom. Magteld's doctor had been due to phone in the afternoon about her appointment, but as darkness fell we had heard nothing. About an hour after coming home I climbed the seventeen steps to the first floor and checked on Adam's room.

The light on the answerphone was blinking. I pressed the 'play' button. The message was from her GP. It was a request to call back.

I called Magteld upstairs and watched as she returned the call. She stood with her back to me, looking out over the back garden where Adam was bouncing on his trampoline in the dim glow of the streetlight. I heard a tremble in Magteld's voice as she spoke to the doctor, and then saw a violent change in her body shape, as if an invisible man had punched her in the stomach.

She blurted out the words: 'Is it bad?'

Even before she ended the call I knew it was worse than bad, horribly worse, and felt my blood freeze in the interminable seconds before she hung up. When she did her voice was crumbling.

'Gordon, what are lesions?' she asked with darkening eyes.

I wasn't sure, but the X-ray had shown up quite a few of them. We were cast back into interpreting the brutally precise language of the medical profession. Whatever they were, they bore no goodwill. I imagined the scan showing a cluster of grey blotches like dead insects.

She let rip with a vile scream of rage, a shriek from the pit of despair that defied her weakening lungs. 'No, I can't die!' She sobbed bitterly, the only real bitterness she ever showed through the whole process.

The doctor booked an appointment with Miss Winter for Wednesday. We were back where we had been eighteen months earlier, drifting into an uneasy sleep and wondering what on earth we were going to tell the children.

For the forty-eight hours before Magteld saw Miss Winter we clutched each other like mountaineers hurtling down a hillside. Hope and fear were rolled up together. Perhaps the 'lesions' weren't full-blown tumours; perhaps they could still be blasted away; perhaps some miraculous new treatment was in development that would allow her to live for years yet. Perhaps, perhaps, perhaps, in a perpetual motion of wistful denial.

At other times I brooded on the cruel binary nature of cancer treatment. The odds mean nothing: you live, and then you die. The tips of Magteld's fingernails were still brittle and yellow from chemotherapy; she had spent months watching the new pink enamel rise from the cuticle.

Her appointment was just after lunchtime. A nurse called us through from the waiting area. As we approached the room I glanced through the doorway and saw Miss Winter preparing herself. Her eyes met mine for a fraction of a second, and in that moment the last thread of hope snapped.

I clasped Magteld's hand a little tighter, gently, soothingly, so as not to alarm her as I led her to the gallows. She would know her fate soon enough.

Miss Winter sat us down. 'Have you not been feeling well?' she asked. Magteld described, in a trembling voice, her wretched persistent cough.

Then came the confirmation. The dark spots in Magteld's lungs were outposts of secondary cancer. All that rigorous treatment, the pain and exhaustion, had brought barely six months' relief.

'We can treat it, but we can't make it go away this time,' Miss Winter said in an apologetic tone. The phrase 'quality of life' marked a shift of emphasis. The first treatment had been focused on cutting out the cancer and restoring the years she was due. Those ambitions were now replaced with lesser, more urgent ones. Miss Winter booked a CT scan, to check if the cancer had spread to other organs, after which Magteld would see Dr Barrett again. 'Come back and see me in three months,' she said finally, and made an appointment for April, a few days before we sailed. At least there was a comfort: that the future could still be measured in months.

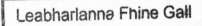

I felt a vapid, gnawing anger and a sense that time was suddenly very precious. Our hopes of a new life together in the Netherlands had been smashed while the ship was still in port. Now Magteld was racing against time to get back for whatever remained of her life. There were twelve weeks left until we set sail for The Hague. Beyond that we would cherish every day that dawned.

In the supermarket that Sunday afternoon Magteld felt something jabbing at her lungs from the inside. It came on rapidly and without warning, like toothache. She sat down in the foyer with Adam while Euan and I finished shopping. By the time I came back she was groaning through clenched teeth. We drove up to the A&E department at the Victoria Hospital with our supper still in shopping bags in the car.

We sat and waited in a row of red plastic seats while a doctor was found. Sunday afternoon was quietly ticking over into evening and the late weekend rush was yet to come. Magteld was called through, placed on a wheeled bed and given an examination. She explained her situation without fuss or alarm. Euan and Adam, too, were remarkably accepting of this sudden deviation from routine. They noted every flinch and grimace, trying to sense their mother's pain. We had not yet mustered the energy or honesty to tell them the dismal truth.

It was likely that the tumour was prodding against the edge of her lung, the doctor declared. He gave her a dose of painkillers and ordered her to be kept in for the night. Dr Barrett had booked her CT scan for the next morning, after which she could go home. Once again I was dispatched to go home and pack an overnight bag. Our next-door neighbour minded the boys as I dashed back out in the rain.

Magteld was put on the emergency ward, on one of the lower floors of the hospital. When I returned and located her she smiled weakly. A trickle of grey light found its way in through the small window of her room, and the corridor echoed to the rhythmic bleep and hum of monitors. The painkillers had blunted the agony and allowed her to recuperate, a little. She was looking forward to getting some sleep and told me not to worry. I pressed a fretful kiss on her lips and went back home.

The next morning she told me about the patient across the corridor, evidently close to death, whose stertorous breathing and rasping cough filled the darkness. What thoughts circled in her mind that night I cannot imagine. She had crossed into that rarefied domain where only the dying are admitted.

In the New Victoria Hospital, in the consultation room where none of us wanted to be, Dr Barrett guided Magteld through the results of the CT scan. Her soft voice was solemn and compassionate. The scan revealed several tumours in one of her lungs and a spot in her liver. Dr Barrett repeated Miss Winter's awful admission of a week ago: all the medical expertise in the world in 2013 had been unable to exorcise the cancer.

Magteld's had been a particularly vicious type; we already knew that the chemotherapy had hardly dented the tumour, but now it seemed the radiotherapy hadn't managed to snuff it out either.

She had followed all the prescriptions: lived healthily, submitted to the withering regimen of chemotherapy and taken her medicine dutifully. None of it counted for anything. Her cancer had withstood a battering, and now it was coming back to destroy her. What doesn't kill you makes you weaker.

'I'm so sorry,' Dr Barrett said.

Magteld faced a new round of chemotherapy. More gruelling treatment, blood tests and enforced sickness, but this time with no hope of recovery. If it worked, she would simply go on taking it until the cancer grew too strong. This was not a battle but a last stand.

The prospects began at terrifying and went up to unbearable. 'If the treatment goes well and the tumour is under control, we might be looking at two to three years,' Dr Barrett said. 'Perhaps longer.'

'And if not?' Magteld asked.

'If it doesn't respond – and there's still lots of things we can do – it could be less than a year.'

We looked at her in dumb silence.

'I'm really sorry,' Dr Barrett said again. Meaning: I'm sorry I can't cure you. I'm sorry medical science isn't the miracle you needed it to be. I'm sorry to be the one to tell you you're going to die young. I'm sorry you will be a dim memory to your children. I'm sorry they're going to watch you suffer.

But she couldn't say any of those things. She gave Magteld a sympathetic smile, and we gathered ourselves up, and booked another appointment for next week, and walked out into the pale sunlight, barely able to feel the ground beneath us.

Now that the horror was roaring in our ears, Magteld started writing her blog again. 'The one thing I was most scared of happened. The cancer had spread to my lungs,' she wrote. 'It felt like we had woken up in a nightmare, but it was really happening.'

A year after she died I met one of her friends for coffee in Glasgow. Claudia had got to know Magteld at Maggie's. Like Magteld, she was an expat, from Germany, and she acknowledged it was a matter of chance that she had survived cancer while Magteld had not. She was one of the first people Magteld told about having 'secondaries'. As the boys played on the swings in Kelvingrove Park, Claudia recalled that conversation. 'She just accepted it,' was her assessment. There was no wailing, no bitterness, no meta-phorical rending of clothes. Bitterness and regret were left to others, like me. Magteld was entirely focused on wringing the minutes from the days. She resolutely declined to learn any further details of her prognosis; she studied her treatment with a microscopic gaze but didn't care to speculate about how long she had left. Death was lurking beneath the window; it could wait a while yet.

In that moment of diagnosis, Magteld entered what the political strategist Philip Gould called the 'death phase'. Gould died in November 2011, three months after receiving his own terminal diagnosis, something he accepted with intimidating clarity. 'The moment you enter the death phase it is a different place,' he said in an interview.* 'It's more intense, more extraordinary, much more powerful.' That is what I think Magteld must have experienced. Life acquired a violent sense of urgency. Most of the time mortality is a vague hum in the background that we only occasionally notice, but in the ears of the dying it rises to a scream. She drew up plans like an architect given a day to build a cathedral. What caught me off guard was the lack of panic. Her urgency was focused, not frantic. It was simply now or never.

She liked to tell a story she had heard of a man whose doctor told him he only had three months to live. 'When he heard that,' she said, 'he looked up from his newspaper and smiled.' The man had been told the same thing, ten years earlier, and was still breathing unimpeded. It wasn't that he thought himself invincible, she explained, but the first experience had cured him of the mania for trying to second-guess fate.

There were regrets, but not for a lost life. 'The thought of not seeing my boys when they become grown men hurts the most,' she wrote. She felt guilt at abandoning the children when the job of raising them, which had consumed her last decade, was still half-finished. She had to trust me to take up the responsibility of caring for them single-handed, in her country. The life we planned was in ruins; all we could do was build another one from the rubble.

I understood, now, why she had resisted seeing the doctor

* *The Guardian*, 20 September 2011; http://www.theguardian.com/politics/2011/sep/20/philip-gould-cancer

about her cough. Though it tormented me at the time, I cannot condemn her for it. She dismissed my entreaties with that flint-like gaze she had sharpened in her dealings with council officials. She hid her fear with the determination of an alcoholic stashing whisky bottles. But there was a logic in wanting to delay the inevitable. She had no desire to spend hours sitting in the doctor's surgery and weeks waiting for test results while her nerves turned to soup. Who would choose to stare into the abyss when a new branch of life is hanging above their heads, bursting with succulent fruit?

The first time we sat down with the boys to talk about cancer the bad news had been wrapped in the protective membrane of hope. The medicine that was going to make mummy very sick would also make her better. This time there was no redeeming balance, no fig leaf, no consolation. She would not be there to watch them grow up, or cycle with them to school, or join them on camping holidays, or share all the other quirks of Dutch life that we had written into our mythical future. All these dreams would rust away like wrecks on the seabed.

So we sat around the kitchen table, just as we had eighteen months before. Magteld talked about her treatment, and then explained that the doctors hadn't been able to cure her. To me her voice seemed eerily calm and firm, because I still didn't understand that she was in the death phase now. Adam, however, seemed to grasp this. When Magteld told them she wouldn't be there for them later, he replied simply,

'But you're here now, Mum.' He was eight and a half. I, more than four times older, was uselessly raging at the injustice of the universe.

Euan offered no visible response at first. But a few days later he went up to Magteld, buried his face in her shoulder and cried silently, leaning into her, yielding to his grief.

Calling off her trip to The Hague was unthinkable. Our house was sold, and we needed to find a new one. Flights had been booked, viewings arranged. Magteld was even more determined than before to see her sisters, especially Marlies, who was eight months pregnant. Life simply had to go on. Moving to Holland was a show of defiance against cancer. What we were supposed to do once we were there, and she was gone, was a question I mostly ignored.

It is the ghastly privilege of the dying to live in a kind of exalted present. As Dennis Potter remarked in his famous TV interview: 'The nowness of everything is absolutely wondrous.' Erasing yourself from the future is wretched, but all the worries about later life – what will happen with my career, have I saved enough for my pension, who will care for me when I am old – suddenly evaporate. You worry not for yourself but for the people you will leave behind. Gordon Aikman, who was diagnosed with Motor Neurone Disease in his late twenties and became a passionate fund-raiser, wrote in *The Scotsman*: 'I have experienced immense pain, but far greater happiness. Dying has taught me how to live.' I'm not sure what use these lessons are to us when we are held captive by the delusion of endless time, but they suggest that our last days will not be as riddled with fear as we tend to think.

As the date of her flight drew nearer, Magteld's cough became worse. Just a few weeks earlier she had bought a running magazine as motivation to start training again in the spring. Now a short walk left her gasping for breath. At the airport she clung to my arm, like a caricature of a doddering grandmother, as I steered her towards the wheelchair we had booked in advance. It was our first experience of the logistical puzzle that travelling becomes when you're disabled.

With the help of a wheelchair, procured by Sanneke, Magteld viewed four houses in The Hague, two of which she swiftly discounted because of their location or condition. I realised we were becoming the pernickety buyers we had cursed when our own house was up for sale. But we had new concerns: Magteld had to consider that she would soon be unable to climb stairs.

It came down to a choice of two. Both in the same neighbourhood, both with bedrooms on the ground floor. Magteld had her sights locked on an *appartement met tussenbouw* – a curious construction that was essentially a ground-floor flat with a garden, but with two upstairs bedrooms, stacked one above the other, up a staircase off the main hall. The courtyard garden was lined with mature trees and the main rooms had high ceilings reminiscent of Glasgow's tenements, creating a sense of light and space. It was close to Adam's school and just over a mile from the beach.

It was a while before I understood how much importance Magteld attached to the task of choosing a house. I instinctively quibbled over everything: did the sellers see a family of incomers as an opportunity to pump up the price? Would our bedroom, which was on the ground floor beside a main road, be too noisy? Was there really enough space? But Magteld was unbending. For her this was a key part of her legacy. On the phone she painted a picture of the street with its tall, elegant trees, the square at the end surrounded by bistros and grocers, the kiosk selling fresh fish and Dutch snacks, the local high street with its famous cheesemonger. When I suggested haggling over the price she replied in a voice that could have cut an electric fence.

I collected her from the airport, wheeled her to the car from the arrival gate and saw how she puffed and grunted as she climbed into the passenger seat. She was seeing Dr Barrett in a few days to begin her next treatment. She had secured a school place for Adam. And now she had found us a house. There were ten weeks to go until we left Scotland, and we were daring to believe we would make it.

Dr Barrett's new chemotherapy plan had the merit of being less intrusive than the first. Magteld was prescribed a drug called xeloda which came in tablet form, so she was spared the ordeal of sitting on the chemo ward with plastic tubes sprouting from her arms. All she had to do was go to the clinic every three weeks, have her bloods tested and collect her drugs in a big paper bag, as if picking up an order from the takeaway.

I had planned to take a few days off at the end of February to go walking in the Highlands, but that was back in the halcyon days of mid-January. Magteld insisted I went ahead with the trip. We both needed space to contemplate. 'I'll cope,' she said.

The xeloda brought rapid relief. Within a week the treatment had extinguished the cough that had rattled her lungs. Like a heavy spring shower that leaves droplets on flowers and the sharp smell of ozone, it felt like a small miracle and gave us fresh hope of achieving our improbable dream.

I stepped off the train in Newtonmore, a tiny unmanned station a mile from the village, with a single track and one platform serving the trains going both ways. I alternated writing with short walks in the hills, nourishing the hopeless aspiration of becoming a self-absorbed pen-chewing recluse. It began with a three-mile tramp to the bed and breakfast I had specifically chosen for its remoteness.

Just before I left, there was an unexpected complication. I'd applied for a job in Utrecht and been offered an interview by video link. The date clashed with my Highland jaunt. I decided to incorporate the interview into my trip. Perhaps having the hills in the background, veiled by a curtain of Highland rain, might give me an advantage. In any case it was a more scenic location than my kitchen or an office in Utrecht.

On the first day, I walked up to the most prominent building in the area, Ruthven Barracks, a colossal ruined fortress on top of an artificial mound. Much of the landscape of the Highlands is an uneasy fusion of natural beauty and man-made monstrosities; the route I took, General Wade's Military Road, was one of several poker-straight highways carved through the mountains to allow soldiers to march north and subdue the unruly glen dwellers. (The barracks were in service for just thirty years before being torched by Bonnie Prince Charlie's retreating army in 1746.)

On day two I set out under the cotton-wool skies that had hung over the hills all week, but as I walked the wispy rain gathered intensity, in that peculiarly Scottish way that gives you the sense of being soaked from the inside, and by the end I was squelching along a farm track as the smirr filled the tractor grooves, my raincoat drenched and my bare legs splattered with mud, descending through the fields to the house just in time to meet the owner on a trip back from the shops. Rarely have I been more grateful for a warm shower.

The interview, on the last morning, made me think that we might, after all, be able to enjoy a regular life in Holland. Magteld was visibly stronger and I had the tantalising prospect of a regular job, with office hours and steady wages. Could that unimaginable luxury, a settled family life, really flourish in such hostile conditions?

The Dutch fetish for precise measurement infiltrates every corner of life. Everything is scrupulously halved and quartered: six months is more usually termed 'a half year', time is measured in top-heavy fractions such as 'five quarters' (for seventy-five minutes), and before the euro replaced the guilder there was a coin, the *rijksdaalder*, which was worth 2½ guilders.

This fastidious attachment to fractions extends to the first major marital milestone, the copper wedding, which marks the 12½-year point. It has some strange repercussions, not least that the anniversary falls in the opposite half of the year from the wedding day. Since we were married on 7 September, ours came around on 7 March, two days after Magteld's thirty-eighth birthday and the day after her parents arrived.

I wanted to surprise her, but recent events had taken the romance out of unpredictability. It was akin to organising a picnic on the beach while a vicious hurricane was tracking across the ocean. But as her cough cleared I took the chance and booked a Sunday night away in Edinburgh. I wove a conspiracy of silence: her parents would take the children to school, and the breast nurse rescheduled her weekly blood test for Tuesday instead of Monday morning. The anniversary had a greater, unwelcome significance now. Years were like passing comets; Magteld's thirty-eighth birthday would almost certainly be her last. I wanted to make it a day to remember. I trawled the Argyll Arcade, an indoor hive of jewellers in the centre of Glasgow, for a suitable necklace. The question had crossed my mind as to what the value of such a trinket was to someone who would only own it for a matter of months. Precious metals represent enduring love, while ours was perishing. We had been robbed of the innocence of eternity. But we could still live and love in this condensed distorted time, this exalted present, and the necklace, like the love it symbolised, would accompany her into the grave. So I proceeded with my shopping mission and hoped that the sales talk wouldn't be too heavily laced with references to lifelong memories.

I gave up trying to explain Dutch anniversaries when the first sales assistant responded with 'Nearly thirteen, then.'

The shops ranged from musty emporiums with black and gold lettered signs, where stooped and waistcoated owners ponderously laid out their wares on green-baize tables, to minimalist, whitewashed establishments with lavender-coloured carpets and glass counters, staffed by sharp-jawed women in pencil-skirted suits. I chose a modern design, a pair of interlocking knots with a trace of Celtic influence, on a white gold chain.

I told her on our actual anniversary, the Friday before. She replied as expected: 'But, Gordon, I have to go to the GP on Monday morning.' Blood tests had supplanted the menstrual cycle as the regulator of her weeks. 'I phoned the nurse,' I said, with a look that said, *See, I thought of everything.* 'You're getting your bloods done on Tuesday.'

Later that day we learned that Marlies had given birth to a baby boy, Maas. We opened a bottle of prosecco with her parents, to celebrate life and love, and glance cautiously at the future, like astronomers watching a flaring sun.

Our trip to Edinburgh had become a farewell to the city where we first lived together, eighteen years earlier. For twenty-four hours we would pretend we were comfortable and carefree – though Magteld would need to sleep in the afternoon to relieve the strain of chemotherapy. Her sleep had been disrupted of late by twinges in her back. And although her cough had dissipated, she was still short of breath and could only walk short distances slowly.

I got my first leg-up in journalism at university, when *The Scotsman* dispatched me to report on second-division rugby games from rickety wooden stands in places like Biggar and Milngavie, where I scribbled in damp-curled notebooks and tried to shut out the November cold that crept in through my socks. In the 1990s the newspaper still had a serious claim to be a national broadsheet and was housed in an eccentric old baronial building, overlooking North Bridge and the miniature canyon that houses Waverley railway station. Several years later, as the newspaper's ambitions diminished, it moved out to a soulless modern hangar next to the Scottish Parliament and handed the keys to its stately seat of power to a hotel developer. And it was in the Scotsman Hotel that Magteld and I celebrated our copper wedding.

Fine cobwebs of rain, rustled by a gentle breeze, were draped over the city as we arrived by first-class train in mid-morning. The Scotsman Steps, the covered stone stairway renovated by Martin Creed with a different mineral, texture and colour on every step, led up from the station to the hotel's front door. Despite Magteld's weakened state and the dreich conditions, we wanted to savour it one last time. Traipsing round Edinburgh's open catacomb of bridges and stairways, cobbles and archways, wynds and closes is one of the city's great pleasures.

I had informed the hotel of Magteld's illness in case she needed help during the night, but also told them it was our anniversary. When we got there we discovered our room had been upgraded to a suite. We took the lift to the top floor, trying to suppress our excitement, like teenagers on a school trip. The lift doors opened and we stepped into our room, with its view across the station's canopies towards the even grander Balmoral Hotel and its giant clock. With the veil of rain drawn across the blue waters of the Firth of Forth, the Balmoral and the monuments of Calton Hill looked especially aloof. But even in the grey gloom it was a sumptuous view.

In the afternoon we picked our way through Princes Street Gardens, huddled together against the cold, picking out the crocuses and the tentative signs of spring. Looping back through the Grassmarket we took lunch at the Last Drop, a staple of our pub-trawling days, where the walls were still clad in the same collage of international banknotes. Here we had toasted the onset of 1997, Magteld's first Hogmanay in her new homeland, with Sanneke and Marlies, and taken shelter on windswept Sunday afternoons with haggis-filled baked potatoes and pints of 80 Shilling. Across the road was Armstrong's, the vintage clothes store, where Magteld picked out a leather jacket and a pair of sunglasses, giving me that squinting goofy look that she used when trying on new accessories, and I bagged a shirt for five pounds.

On we went, up the winding slope of Victoria Street, pausing for breath by the window of a secondhand bookshop, then on to the Royal Mile, past brooding old St Giles' Kirk and the High Court, where I had once joined the swarm of reporters outside the door, shouting the verdicts of murder trials into their phones. Up and down the street were signs advertising ghost walks: historical tours led by students in fancy dress to monetise the city's folklore. Further along was the Filling Station, the ageless cocktail bar where Magteld had celebrated her twenty-first birthday with a small party of friends.

I gave her my arm as we staggered down the News Steps, up Market Street and down another flight of steps to the Scottish National Gallery. Though she was tiring by now, Magteld wanted to step into the gallery one last time. We had been here a few weeks into her first chemotherapy for an exhibition titled 'Van Gogh to Kandinsky'. The title was a little misleading, as there was only one Van Gogh on show – *The Sower* – and two Kandinskys, but their absence was compensated by less-lauded gems, such as the deceptively naturalistic work of the Scandinavians. A sunset landscape by the Finnish artist Albert Edelfelt stood out for its unmitigated stillness – the lake as smooth as a glacier, the treetops submerging in their own shadows, and not a hint of habitation by human, bird or beast. Its sense of peace and permanence was deeply consoling at a time when our own lives felt so fragile. Another Edelfelt work depicted a dead tree with huge splinters jagging out of its split trunk, amid a forest of timid, upright young saplings, containing both the transience and the resilience of life in a single image. Now the building itself offered solace in its elegant symmetry, the arrangement of paintings and the soft movement of visitors circling the galleries in studied appreciation.

Back at the hotel Magteld sank into the large soft bed, while I perused the little pile of books on the side table. I picked out a volume of essays by F.R. Leavis and went through to the living room, with its darkening view of the Princes Street skyline. I slung on a CD of Mahler's First Symphony, with its stirring final movement marked

Stürmisch bewegt – agitated, as by a storm – and absorbed myself for a precious hour in music and literature.

When Magteld awoke I gave her the necklace. 'You didn't have to do that,' she said, but how many more chances would I have to make her feel special? We changed and went downstairs for dinner. She was wilting, and the pain in her spine was rising again, but she soothed it with a glass of wine and made it to dessert.

We climbed into bed, exhausted and relieved. Magteld had the pillows plumped up to support her back, but in the middle of the night she woke in discomfort, got up and walked through to the living-room window. The rain had stopped, the clouds had drifted away and Edinburgh's vertiginous skyline was lit up by a canopy of stars. It seemed to quieten her. She came back to bed and we nestled together for a while, intimately, defying the malingering proximity of death, before floating back off to sleep.

By morning her pain had subsided. We had breakfast in what used to be the *Scotsman*'s reception area, then took the lift down to the station, through the back entrance where bundled stacks of newspapers had once been flung out of the door and loaded on to waiting trains. We headed back to Glasgow in our first-class carriage, which felt as if it would turn into a pumpkin once we got out at Central Station and rejoined the flow of time.

'You two look radiant,' Diny said as we arrived home.

Magteld had seen the doctor on her birthday about the pain in her spine. The diagnosis was a torn shoulder, an injury more commonly seen in rugby players, and she was given an appointment with a physiotherapist. The violent coughing was the most likely culprit, and now that was gone her shoulder would probably recover with therapy. She was happily surprised: 'At last, something that's not caused by cancer.'

The pain, however, tightened like a thumbscrew. At first Magteld found it awkward to lift her arms above her head, but after a few weeks she could barely raise them above elbow height. I remember her putting away plates in an overhead cupboard, gritting her teeth and swinging her arms upwards so the momentum would carry them to eye level. The muscles in her upper arms felt tight and knotted and the nerves in her fingers were desensitised. It was becoming harder for her to hold a pen, and her handwriting became cramped and spidery, like an old man's. The pain seemed to follow a daily cycle, peaking in the small hours of the night. Magteld would wake in agony and get out of bed, hoping to stretch her spine so she would not have to resort to painkillers. At the worst moments she would cry out in the darkness, 'Kill me now!', and I would leap up, alarmed, not daring to hold her, and try to lead her back to the warmth of the bed. Only when the pangs had ground her into submission would she relent and let me fetch the bottle of pills from the kitchen.

One morning at breakfast Adam said, 'Mum, in the night I heard you crying.'

There were less than seven weeks to go now until we boarded the ferry. The days stretched and yawned, buds appeared on the trees, the boys had just a fortnight left in school. Luc and Diny flew back to Amsterdam to see their new grandchild, Maas, and then went away for a weekend to walk part of the West Highland Way. Luc and I, both keen distance runners, signed up for the Nigel Barge 10k race in Glasgow at the end of March. Over the years we had run several road races together, including two trips to Islay for the island's half-marathon, sponsored by a distillery, where the competitors are treated at the finish to whisky and sandwiches in Bowmore village hall.

Magteld nurtured fantasies of our new life in The Hague: taking the tram to the beach, walking the winding paths through the dunes, with the murmur of the North Sea on one side and the buzz of the city, close by but seemingly distant, on the other. That sense of bliss and balance, the rhythm of walking, the vividness of the sky and the sharp salty smell of the sea – it was all the paradise she needed.

Just as I had all but given up on hearing any more about the job I had applied for, I was invited for a second interview. There were two candidates left, and I would have to travel to Utrecht. Privately I had assumed that the end of the first interview, when I explained that my wife was terminally ill and I was her main carer, had signalled the end of my chances. And now the dream was back on.

I sat down to book a flight to Amsterdam. The interview was the following Tuesday. I would spend two nights with Sanneke and Sjoerd, with the unexpected bonus of being able to see the house I'd just bought. I clicked through the menus, selecting the cheapest flight: hand luggage only, no hotel, no insurance. Then I filled in my passport details. A message flashed up: 'Your passport expiration date is before the date of the flight. Please check and try again.'

I looked in my passport. The red booklet had been defunct for three weeks. And then I remembered: before Christmas I'd made a mental note that I needed to renew Euan's passport before it ran out in mid-February.

Magteld's organisational instinct kicked in. 'You need to drop everything else and sort this out,' she said. Mercifully Glasgow had a passport office which offered a fast-track service – at a premium rate – for disorganised idiots. That meant I could go to Utrecht, but the high-speed option wasn't available for children, and a regular passport application took around six weeks to process.

Our boat was sailing in less than seven weeks.

Looking back, it seems almost laughable to suggest this was the biggest threat to our plans at the time, but that's how it felt. I acquired a new passport for myself the next day, dispatched the form for Euan's, and resigned myself to a nerve-shredding wait.

The following Monday I viewed the house for the first time. Magteld's house, the place where she had chosen to die. The owners were busy, like us, squeezing their lives into boxes. It was bigger than it looked in the brochure, with the bedrooms in a wing off the main hall and sliding glass doors between the two downstairs rooms so that they could form one large space for entertaining. The courtyard garden was lined with raised beds that were planted up with mature trees, so that from indoors the thick foliage gave the impression of a tropical clearing. I imagined what it would be like on a warm summer's night, full of people, bursting with life and laughter, as the children retreated to their annexe. She had chosen well.

'I may not have a long life, but I have a good life,' Magteld wrote, a week after learning she would not grow old.

Talking about death is never easy, and talking about the imminent demise of somebody you love, when they're sitting having coffee with you in the kitchen is almost unthinkable. The writer Michel Faber, whose wife Eva died of multiple myeloma around the same time as Magteld, put it like this: 'When your partner is dying of a disease that you don't have and you know that you are going to outlive her, they are on a different planet. They've already gone somewhere where you can't follow.'

Magteld rarely gave in to fear or self-pity. When we lived in Edinburgh she had once burst into tears spontaneously on a bus and told me she didn't believe in happiness. Yet in her last days she was serenely calm for the most part. I wondered if she only felt able to be truly, unconditionally happy in the final stages. She never regretted the past, only the lost future.

She prepared her final scene carefully, but when she raised it in conversation she was studiedly casual, as if describing a temporary setback. She knew how she wanted to be at the end and set it out clearly: in her own home, preferably in her own bed, with her three boys – Euan, Adam and me – beside her. Nobody else. I nodded. Silence enveloped us for a moment. Then she looked up, clutched my hand and gave me that familiar smile.

I hated the fact that I couldn't be with Magteld in the place she had gone to in her mind. She lived in the exalted present; the best I could do was suspend my belief in the future. More troubling was the growing awareness that she was protecting me from it. I didn't belong there. Dying is something you have to face alone, even in the midst of people you love. She had an instinct to spare me, and the boys, from the empty terror.

Only once can I remember her letting her guard down. We were sitting at the kitchen table in Glasgow, going over her last wishes, when she looked across at me and said, 'I won't feel it, will I? The eternal blackness?'

I hesitated a second. 'I don't know,' I said. I fumbled for words that might reassure. 'It won't hurt. I don't think it will.'

I reached across and grasped her warm, trembling fingers, and she smiled and rubbed my hands.

8

Running was my relief, and during Magteld's treatment I relied on it even more. Not so much for the endorphin rush, of whose benefits I've never really been convinced, but because of the discipline and sense of rhythm it bestows. Cordoning off an hour of the daily schedule to disconnect from smartphones, rolling news and the whole plastic soup of modern life was like visiting an oasis of pure time. Often I thought of nothing more than the rhythm of my feet slapping the wet paving stones or the steady slope up to Newton Mearns or the numbers on my stopwatch. But when I got home I found myself calmer, nimbler and more decisive. An hour dashing through the streets typically generated two or three more productive ones later in the day.

Once Magteld's treatment resumed, there were fewer opportunities to go running, and often I set out feeling a sense of displaced guilt that I could still exercise unrestricted. I was also dogged by the fear that her health would take a drastic turn while I was away. Every time an ambulance flashed by I would track the fading trail of its blue lights to see if it was heading towards the house.

One Tuesday afternoon I set off on my regular run to the Mearns shopping centre, a four-mile shallow climb through Glasgow's southern suburbs and back home again. The pain and numbness in Magteld's spine had spread to her forearms, and she was barely able to raise her arms above the elbow. The physiotherapist, whom she had seen the previous week, was unconvinced by the GP's explanation of a torn shoulder and referred her to the hospital for a scan.

My run took around an hour. When I got back Magteld was standing at the foot of the stairs, her face screwed up in distress.

'Gordon, you've got to take me to the hospital,' she said in a quavering voice. The pain had engulfed her so quickly in the past hour that she had phoned the NHS advice line and been told to go straight to A&E. It was a key-change moment.

The next hour is a blur. I can't remember if I managed a shower or simply threw on my tracksuit and jumped into the car. Somebody must have come round to mind the boys, because they weren't with us when we got to the hospital. I led Magteld out to the car, feeling how she juddered with every step as if she was walking barefoot across a bed of thistles. I have no recall of where we went when we got to the hospital, or at what point a bed was found for her, or how I explained it to the children.

She did not climb those stairs ever again, or take another step unaided. And she would not catch the ferry to Holland with us at the end of the month.

The next day, on the hospital ward, she was sitting up in bed, supported by two pillows to protect her spine. Her movement was restricted to her lower arms and neck. If she tried to get up and walk now, the nurses warned, her legs would collapse under her.

Two days later an ambulance took her across the city to the Beatson for an MRI scan. That would tell her what convulsions were going on in her body. Her father followed in convoy in his car, while I stayed at home with the boys. Afterwards she was transported back to her bed in the Victoria Infirmary. The whole round trip lasted several uncomfortable hours.

We had the results from Dr Barrett in the morning. The xeloda had failed. It had eased the inflammation in her lungs but not slowed the cancer's progress. It was a crushing blow, a cruel deception. The tumours had rampaged up and down her spine and ripped into her nervous system. The cancer had not stopped at her back but marched on into her liver. Her cells were in full mutiny.

There was still hope, Dr Barrett insisted, but I saw a trace of shock in her face that hadn't been there before. Even the most experienced cancer specialist cannot be unmoved by the sight of a once healthy young woman imploding despite your fervent efforts to save her. Magteld wanted to know everything, except for one detail: she still refused to hear her exact prognosis.

She would have a short course of radiotherapy, four rapid blasts to try to unfreeze her spine and contain the spread of the tumours. Dr Barrett advised her to fly out to Holland as soon as possible after that so she could begin a new course of treatment. It was four weeks until the ferry sailed, but even that was too long to wait now.

After speaking to Magteld, Dr Barrett took me into a side room. Together we scoured websites of hospitals in The Hague, looking up colleagues she could communicate with. She needed my help to navigate the Dutch information.

'You need to get her over there as soon as you can,' she said. 'Once you get to The Hague you may only be looking at a very few weeks.'

I nodded mutely. I think I thanked her.

It was Tuesday, 1 April. Back home I booked Magteld and her mother on to a flight to Amsterdam the following Monday. Luc would put her luggage in the car and take it across on the ferry. I rebooked our crossing: Euan and Adam could join her the following week, then I would fly back to Glasgow, finish packing the house and leave Scotland by plane on 25 April. That was the date we had marked for our departure back in January, in a different epoch. The smiley face Magteld had drawn in the diary now seemed to mock me, like a gargoyle, from the page.

From this point on Magteld's decline was precipitous. She went downhill like a runaway mine cart. Time itself seemed to metastasise and lose its integrity. When I came to write this memoir and tried to put the pieces together it was like reassembling a shattered teacup. Her blogs, our Facebook entries, records of flights and hotel bookings, the diaries where she logged her hospital appointments – all conflicted with the jumbled shards in my mind. For instance, to my recollection she went into hospital a few days after we came back from Edinburgh, but the records showed there was a two-week ceasefire in between, which was blurred out in the chaos that followed.

Even so, I don't recall any sense that she was hurtling towards the end. Had we been aware how compressed our time was becoming we might have wasted it in a mindless panic.

It was important for the boys to maintain as much of their routine as possible. Luc and Diny were with me most evenings, cooking and covering. Euan was rehearsing for a show to mark his school's fiftieth anniversary, in which he and three classmates were performing as The Beatles. Magteld's hopes of watching him had been blown away by cancer, but at least Euan had something to focus on.

As I walked back with him from his Scout group one night I tried to explain why his mum was not at home. She was in hospital, I said, and would be staying there a few more nights so the doctors could look after her.

'Does that mean she won't come to our house any more?' he asked without looking at me.

I could have disintegrated on the spot. 'Your mum loves you,' I said, spluttering the words. There were more days like this to come, I knew, and no sheltering from them.

Gordon Aikman described how 'the progressive nature of [Motor Neurone Disease] means that as soon as you adapt to one challenge, another is tapping you on the shoulder'. Cancer is usually a more gradual disease than MND, which must feel like having your body stripped of its wiring from the inside. But in Magteld's case the comparison was apt: no sooner had she adjusted to her reduced lung capacity than the tumours mounted an assault on her spinal column. Two weeks earlier she had walked home from the physiotherapy clinic, a mile away. Now the nurses at the Beatson were having to scramble a wheelchair for her so she could be discharged. She needed specially moulded cutlery to guide her weakened hands to her mouth, and a grabber tool to reach things she could no longer stretch for.

When I visited her on the Sunday she was being taught to walk with a Zimmer frame. One slippered foot on the ground, then a little shuffle, then a deep, hissing intake of breath and a careful shove forward with the frame. Five minutes of this brought her to the other side of the room, where she rewarded herself by sinking into a chair.

Even now, though, she refused to bow her head. We went upstairs together to the Friends of the Beatson room, run by a respite charity similar to Maggie's. There were jigsaws and games for the boys, books and magazines and a television. Magteld had her hair cut. It was a small but vital acknowledgement of her humanity. As soon as she came home she posted her blog again. 'I'm not fighting cancer, as it's impossible to fight against your own body,' she wrote. 'I'm living and enjoying every second of it. So I'm not losing a battle, but making the most of it.'

What followed was more like a heist movie than the preparations for someone's last weeks. Magteld was flying to Holland on Monday, but we wouldn't get the keys to the house for another week and three weeks of renovation work were lined up before we could move in. We had five days to find somewhere for a terminally ill, wheelchair-using cancer patient to live and die, in a different country.

Sanneke set about investigating options in The Hague. She found the Jacobshospice, an intimate six-bed care facility where nurses and a rolling army of volunteers worked to take the strain out of dying.

The word hospice was as sharp and heavy as a guillotine blade. This was not how Magteld had planned her exit. But there was no alternative. I looked at the Jacobshospice website with her: a procession of soothing slow-motion videos, with graceful images and a rocking-chair voice-over. Magteld wept as she watched it. 'It's all old guys,' she said, seething again at the way she been catapulted into life's final phase, dependent on others to move, dress, wash and feed herself, and with oblivion on the horizon.

Sanneke messaged me. There was a room available in the hospice, but to qualify for it Magteld had to have a prognosis of three months or less. Being a Dutch institution, they needed a signed declaration from a medical professional.

'I don't think that's going to be a problem,' I replied.

I gave Dr Barrett Sanneke's email address so she could arrange the documents and feed the paperwork chimera. The next day Magteld's place in the hospice was confirmed. When she arrived on Monday night she would have a room to die in.

The Beatson staff wanted Magteld to stay in hospital until she flew out on Monday afternoon. She could spend the time learning how to use her wheelchair and practise with her new disability cutlery set. Magteld, however, intended to have a weekend with her family. She was as unbending as a medieval martyr who feels the executioner's sword swoop down on the back of their neck.

Some rapid improvisation was required. She could no longer climb the stairs, so we would sleep on the sofabed in the living room, which was only really wide enough for one and a half people. The bathroom was also upstairs, so I had to source a commode from the Red Cross. We also needed to install a ramp at the front door. I was quickly learning the hard truth about disability: every journey, even from the street to the front door, is a negotiation. For all the city's experience with chronic ill health, nowhere in the million-strong conurbation of Greater Glasgow could we find a mobility ramp at short notice. In desperation I procured two long planks from the local DIY store, nailed them to a shorter piece and draped them over the door frame. Once her four days of radiotherapy finished on Friday morning, Magteld could come home.

She took one look at the flimsy wooden ramp, already sagging with the burden of two days' incessant rain, and demanded to be lifted over the threshold. Luc and I grunted and lifted the chair. We had lunch, washed down with a glass of prosecco. 'A toast to life,' said Magteld. She spent the weekend confined to the house and received no visitors. The Glaswegian spring weather was on her side, sending her off with a week-long downpour. A few neighbours rang the doorbell or stopped me in the street, but Magteld refused to meet them in her weakened state. I had to tell them that they would not see her again.

We slept together in the living room, with the commode skulking in the corner. Magteld had a cornucopia of pills to take, including laxatives to counter the combined effect of the anti-inflammatory drugs and her immobility. I had to get used to manoeuvring her from the chair to the bed, swinging her legs in and then rolling her across so she could lie beside me. In the night I had to reverse the procedure in semi-darkness every time she needed the toilet. The laxatives made this a not infrequent occurrence. Then I ran upstairs in a daze to the bathroom to empty the pot. Three nights went by like this. During the daytime we packed bags, watched television and chatted.

Adam despised the commode. He scowled at it like a cat eyeing a new pet hamster. It had an imitation leather seat to make it resemble a regular chair, but like cheap plastic surgery or black hair dye on a leathered face, the facade only highlighted the thing it was trying to conceal. Adam went over to it, flipped up the seat to reveal the plastic tub, replaced the seat, sat on it as if testing its sturdiness, and resumed scowling, without speaking a word. The commode represented the drastic way his mother had become disabled, and Adam hated her disability. So did I. All the entreaties in the world to look beyond the disability and value the person couldn't soften the reality. When I tried to look past her dysfunctional legs, or felt the knobbly lumps in her spine,

I saw cancer gnawing away at her. I didn't want to make space for it or be positive about it. I wanted to destroy it.

Sometimes I couldn't avoid asking myself how long this exhausting torment would last. When I woke in the night to fetch her painkillers, or a glass of water, I felt a sense of resentment swell in the fog of broken sleep. I wanted to care for the woman I loved, but there were other, less generous emotions. A future was coming which contained only the boys and me, with Magteld as a memory hanging on the walls. Sometimes it was easier to think about this than attend to the day-to-day demands of lifting a sick, diminished version of my wife in and out of bed and fetching her medicines. But these were the wages of love, the agreement I had made in gentler times, to love and cherish her, in sickness and in health, till death us did part.

In an alternative future we stood together on the deck of the ferry, holding hands in the morning sunlight as our new homeland materialised on the horizon, barely rising above the lilting waves. In reality Magteld left Glasgow in a black cab, like a villain expelled from a soap opera, accompanied by her mother.

Luc had left in the morning to catch the ferry, taking Magteld's luggage with him. All being well, she and Diny would touch down in Amsterdam before the boat had left port. She travelled light, taking a handbag stuffed with bottles of pills and an explanatory note from the doctor.

For the next eight days we would be separated by the North Sea again. We had email now, and perhaps she could rig up Skype in the hospice, but the gap had never felt so wide. It was a calculated gamble that neither of us would speak of but that her croaky voice and hacksaw-like breathing wouldn't let us forget.

It was still raining as the taxi pulled up outside the door. I wheeled her up, over the ramp and backwards through the front door, affording her a last look at the house as she retreated down the pathway. The driver wheeled her up the ramp and strapped her in. As she cast one last glance at her former home, with its teeming hive of memories, I clutched her limp arms and pressed my lips tightly against hers. As the doors slid shut I thought, this kiss will be separated from the next by eight days and several hundred miles of cold, churning water. Then the driver pulled away and the taxi dissolved into the black rain until only its red tail lights, hovering above the roadway, remained.

Part Two

The Hague

9

Magteld phoned from the Jacobshospice the same evening, while I was making supper. Her voice was hushed, as if she was alone in a candlelit room. She was tired from travelling: a flight unique among the dozens she had made, in which she had to be carried on and off the plane on a trolley. A disability taxi took her and Diny straight to the hospice. Sanneke greeted her, clutching a bottle of prosecco. It was a ceremonial journey, like a pilgrimage, carefully planned and laden with symbolism. She would not see Scotland again. She would not see Sleen again. It was far from certain she'd see the house she'd found us again. I wasn't even sure she'd see me again.

She described her room, which had an en-suite bathroom and an annexe with a desk and a guest bed. 'Everyone's lovely here,' she said, and her voice sounded less strained than it had done for several weeks. The anticipation of the journey, the fear she would be too sick to travel, had dissipated.

The next morning we spent a frustrating hour trying to make video contact on her iPad. As the failures mounted up, her emails became terser and silted up with exclamation marks, until she gave up and we opted for a daily phone call. She was sleeping more in the daytime, like a toddler, as the effort of holding off the cancer exhausted her, so we settled into a routine of speaking mid-morning. Every day I heard her voice, I felt I was pulling myself a little closer towards her on a long chain. Through the day I sent her pictures of the boys and little comments by email. How had we managed, twenty years earlier, to distil our love into one chaste hand-written letter a week?

At home there was a week to fill, a house and a history to be dismantled and packed away. My father was spending a few days in Glasgow, and my cousins were driving up from York at the weekend to help with the packing. The children had finished school, and I had worked my last shift. There was no time to be bored or fearful.

Her emails were staccato and excitable, like postcards from someone whose sight has been restored after years of darkness. She told me about shopping trips with Sanneke, local cafes she had discovered, meals out with her parents. Being an international city, The Hague had an enviable range of takeaways and she wanted to try them all: Portuguese, Nepalese, Surinamese, Thai, Bulgarian. A favourite Riesling was on standby in the fridge. She ordered books for the iPad her parents had bought for her birthday: *The Great Gatsby*, *Bridget Jones*, *Anna Karenina*. She was challenging death, testing whether it had the nerve to snatch her away in the middle of Tolstoy.

Marlies drove across from Arnhem with one-month-old Maas, so Magteld could see and hold her nephew. In a photograph from the hospice she is waving a toy giraffe and gazing down at him, her eyes sparkling with joy. When Euan was born, Magteld's grandfather was dying of cancer. Luc and Diny visited us at my parents' house in Norwich and made a home video of their grandchild. Opa had been told his cancer was untreatable while Magteld was pregnant, but he was determined to live long enough to see Euan. He managed another month. His granddaughter would live barely a decade more.

My father went home in midweek, leaving me alone with the boys for forty-eight hours until my cousins arrived. We went to the Transport Museum, their favourite day out in Glasgow, made lunch and supper and kept on filling boxes. I tried to block the thought that it was a trial balloon for single parenthood.

It was hard to know if Euan and Adam missed their mother. They didn't seem concerned about her absence, or the house being decanted into packing cases: pictures vanishing from walls, shelves drained of books, the stock of toys depleting. It was hard to keep things normal and familiar. Euan was spending the last two nights at respite, which gave me time to pack up his bedroom. Over in The Hague Luc and Diny had booked a beach house for the first two weeks, where we would stay while the house was being renovated. I worried about how the boys would handle this itinerant lifestyle, but on the surface, at least, they seemed unperturbed. I told them they would see their mum soon and focused their attention on their imminent seafaring adventure.

Magteld's voice on the phone sounded more robust and confident with every passing day. Was I imagining it, or was she pausing less often to catch her breath?

While she was in the Victoria Infirmary Magteld had got to know Pauline, a young woman with learning difficulties who had very little speech and was dying of cancer. Nobody apart from the nurses ever came to see her. It was hard to gauge how much she understood about her fate, but Magteld had managed to break through her anxiety and form a kind of friendship. She had garnered that Pauline was interested in knitting patterns, and as we sat in the dining room before she left Glasgow, Magteld gave me an errand.

'I want you to buy a couple of knitting magazines and take them in to her,' she said. Selfless, attentive and practical: a gesture that epitomised how she dealt with people.

I bought the magazines from a newsagent by the hospital, just before evening visiting. I chose two, one of which came in a plastic bag with a free set of needles. At the reception I began a faltering explanation of what I was doing. Thankfully Magteld had briefed the nurses before leaving hospital, and they escorted me down the ward.

Pauline was sitting in a chair by her bed. She flinched a little when I approached her. I tried to explain who I was and why Magteld had sent me. I produced a magazine from the bag and held it out to her. She nodded hurriedly with half-gritted teeth. The whole scene felt like one of those scenes in a Victorian period drama where the earnest, well-meaning hero visits an orphanage for the first time and realises how far he has stepped outside his circle of privilege. However good my intentions, I didn't have Magteld's capacity to reach people. Perhaps I needed more time.

I left the magazines piled on her bedside table and said goodbye. The nurses at the desk told me they would help her open the packages. I hoped it would calm her to sit in her chair, clacking her needles and spinning out the patterns in defiance of fate.

After dropping off Euan at respite, I spent all of Saturday with my cousins, packing up his bedroom and the kitchen. On Sunday morning we went into Glasgow, for the last time as inhabitants, to drink coffee and buy Adam a toy. Then we packed the bags to take with us in the car to Holland. All week I had focused on the ferry journey and distracting the children from what we faced on the other side.

Adam was already wide awake when I went into his bedroom on Monday morning. 'Ready for the boat?' I asked. An excited grin spread across his face.

We fetched Euan from the respite house. He was clutching a balloon from his farewell party the night before. His face, too, was a mask of excitement. What a privilege of youth, I thought, to be able to quit your native city without a pang of remorse.

We went home and gathered up the suitcases. It was eleven o'clock; we were due in Newcastle in around six hours, which gave us a good margin. The next day I was signing the contract for the house at the lawyer's office in The Hague at lunchtime. Everything was set.

With the boys and bags in the car, I decided to give the tyre pressures one last check. As I tugged at the valve there was a loud hissing sound and the dial on the pressure gauge plummeted to zero. Somehow I had contrived to tear a hole in the rubber, and air was flooding out. I looked at the slumped tyre in raw panic. Were all our delicate plans to founder at this stage because of some overzealous pumping?

There was a garage a mile away, beside the Battlefield monument and the Old Victoria Hospital. I pumped the tyre as full as I could and set off, hoping the air would not expire too quickly. I explained the situation to the mechanic, who looked at me slightly wearily, glued the valve shut and wished us on our way. The setback cost us thirty frantic minutes.

The mood was more relaxed when we stopped for lunch by the English border. Gasps of wind shot across the hillside and blew fat clouds across the sky, allowing the occasional flicker of sunlight to steal through. We sat and ate sandwiches on the Scottish side while watching a flock of sheep in England trot through the rippling grass. Technically, now, the boys were migrants in transit. I was not, since I was flying back five days later to tie up the removal and wouldn't emigrate for another ten days. It was a disorienting experience, but we were getting used to weaving new plans from scraps and loose threads, each new structure a little flimsier than the one it replaced.

The sea was stirred by a benign wind, the kind that rocks you to sleep rather than shakes you out of it. I had ordered drinks and snacks in the cabin. Emigration should be marked with some kind of ceremony, I felt, even one as mundane as snapping open a cold beer, a couple of soft drinks and a packet of crisps. When we woke I discovered the sea breeze had delayed the journey by an hour. I took the boys out on deck and we watched the Dutch coastline loom sluggishly into view. We finally rolled off the boat in IJmuiden harbour at eleven o'clock; my appointment at the lawyer's office, an hour and a half's drive away, was scheduled for half past twelve.

The office was tucked away in The Hague's outer suburbs, between glass-fronted shops and solid blonde-brick apartments. Our agent was waiting in the street when the satellite navigation system delivered us to the front door with ten minutes to spare. Luc and Diny were there, too, and took the boys off to the beach house while I went inside.

In Scotland all the paperwork is carried out before a house is sold, and the keys are typically collected in a second-hand brown envelope from the solicitor's reception desk. The Dutch arrangement is more ritualised, with buyer and seller required to sign the contract under a notary's watchful eye. We were ushered into a reception room with a plush claret-coloured carpet and took our seats at a round table. A secretary served coffee while we waited for the notary. The sellers, a divorced couple, were already seated, with their agent strategically placed between them. Throughout the half-hour session the ex-husband gazed straight ahead through pale, bird-like eyes set into his crimson-speckled face, while his former partner led the conversation. Everybody was dressed in jackets and creased trousers, as if for jury service or a friend's graduation.

The notary, a bespectacled man with a thicket of black hair and the pursed-lipped inscrutability of the Dutch professional classes, arrived with a bundle of papers and sat down, dividing the documents into two neat piles. On top was a copy of the first owner's deposition from 1928, written in a slanting wave-like scrawl that had been rendered illegible by the passing years.

He noted Magteld's absence and explained I would have to buy the house in my own name, as she was not available to sign. A little procedural change was required. The sellers nodded their consent, the secretary was summoned and the contract taken away for correction.

In the meantime the notary read through the contract in a dry, even tone, covering the properties of the house, the fees and charges. Then he solemnly asked if we were willing to proceed with the sale. Only when we had said yes was the house officially sold. The secretary scuttled back into the room and placed the amended contract on top of one of the piles of papers. The notary uncapped a fountain pen from his top pocket, signed the document and passed the pen round the table. Once it was back in his hand the owner took the keys from her handbag and passed them across the table to me: three shining steel slabs. There was a little ripple of applause as she congratulated me and shook my hand. I shook hands, too, with the bird-man, who screwed his mouth into an off-smile and muttered his congratulations.

I thanked the estate agent, stepped out into the sunshine and drove off to the beach house to fetch the boys. It was time to rejoin Magteld.

The Jacobshospice was on Koningin Emmakade, in a redbrick canalside terrace adorned with a ribbon of little gables, with marzipan-striped facades that gleamed in the sunlight. Cyclists swooshed past on one side of the road while trams glided along on the other, separated from the canal by a tight row of trees. It was an unmistakably Dutch scene, with its straight lines and neat brickwork and segregated traffic streams. We stepped into a hallway where the light streamed in from above, and from there into the lounge where Magteld was sitting in her wheelchair.

I reached down to kiss her, felt her spindly fingers crawl up my arms and held her as tight as I dared. Eight days had never seemed so long. Her grimace melted, and her urgent breathing eased a little. Her voice was a little stronger, as I had sensed on the phone, but there was a tension in the way she clutched at me that signalled all was not well.

She clutched the boys warmly and kissed them with relief. 'Nice to see you, Mum,' said Adam. It sounded like a cursory greeting, but I knew it meant more, since Adam didn't normally do social graces. He and Euan went over to the sofa, where their eyes had been drawn by three enormous teddy bears, and Magteld gestured to me to wheel her into the hallway so we could talk.

She started sobbing quietly, forcing the breaths from her dilapidated lungs. 'Gordon, I lost a friend,' she said in a soft croak.

The hospice was a blissful place in many ways, where residents were treated as guests and encouraged to read, talk, eat and socialise. It had a library and a garden, and volunteers who would stop for a five-minute chat that lasted half an hour or spontaneously produce a sumptuous banquet for all to share. I felt a stronger sense of life there, among the dying, than exists in many an office or airport or hotel lobby. But there was no way of masking its essential function. Every few evenings a bedroom door would stand open, and a candle would be lit in the hallway, and another resident would silently depart.

Magteld had told me on the phone about Ilse, an elderly woman who was one of her fellow guests. She was in the advanced stages of cancer, and she and Magteld were close friends within a day. They could discuss life and death without inhibition or alarm. They were comrades resisting death, like people who shut their eyes and hold hands before jumping from a moving train. The day before, while the boys and I were hurtling across northern England to catch our ferry, the two of them were sitting chatting with one of the volunteers, until Ilse retired for a nap. They would reconvene over supper.

Ilse never woke up.

And Magteld was confronted once again with the

delicateness of the thread on which all her hopes now hung. Grief and terror floated to the surface. Grief especially: somebody she had connected with so profoundly, in such a precious short time, was gone. And she was left behind, alone, with the death knell clanging in her ears.

I spent my first night in The Hague on the fold-down guest bed in Magteld's hospice room. Manoeuvring her into the low bed was a delicate operation, but it was worth it to be able to feel her warmth and solidity in the night. I woke before dawn and heard the hum of street sweepers maintaining the city's orderliness, then drifted off again to the rhythm of my wife's breathing. We were physically closer in many ways now I had to lift her in and out of her chair several times a day. Her fingers crawled up my arms to gain purchase on my shoulders. Right to the end she retained a vestigial sensuality. Her shallow breath would catch the back of my neck, and we performed a slow, ungainly pas de deux as I lowered her into the chair. Within days the clean-and-jerk procedure of holding her as she stepped into the chair and levering her down became a smooth, practised action.

The physics of our relationship changed. My upper arms and shoulders gained in tone and heft as they adjusted to the demands of shifting Magteld in and out of her wheelchair. I showered her in the en-suite bathroom, washing her limp hair and running the flannel over her knobbly spine, redundant legs and the ruins of her breasts. Her light, playful smile eclipsed the devastation cancer had wrought.

Beneath the window in the annexe was her desk, overlooking the canal, where she wrestled with fat dossiers on cancer treatment and organised the boys' schooling. There was a pile of folders on one side: her medical records, envelopes from the schools and advisory leaflets on hiring a childminder. Here she would sit, scrawling notes in a book, perusing papers or making phone calls, looking up occasionally as a tram whistled past. In a place where people come to die, she was working to secure her family's future. She was a supernova, bursting with brightness and energy in her dwindling last moments.

I regretted that for so long I had failed to make her feel wanted. To me Magteld became more beautiful in her thirties, as she acquired inner strength and self-confidence. I loved her better when she had learned to love herself. Here in the hospice, we curled up together on her sofa like besotted teenagers and snatched kisses in the lift on the way from her room to the dining area. Actual lovemaking was too precarious, though she never gave up hope.

The Dutch newspaper columnist Klaas ten Holt, who lost his wife Bibian to cancer, described how in the aftermath he had to fight the urge to call up the first woman he could think of 'in the hope that she'll stay with me and keep me from this debilitating loneliness'.* All through Magteld's illness, and especially in the days after she died, I often felt like jumping into the arms of the nearest female friend and

* Klaas ten Holt's columns were collected and published in 2014 as *De complete weduwnaar* (*The Complete Widower*)

pleading with her to take me away from all this horror. And I can see how that might have been misinterpreted. Yet once she was gone, the idea of someone else lying on her side of the bed was too discordant. I'd read of widows who'd smothered their loss in sexual escapades, but when the moment came grief crushed my desire like a vice. Magteld had tried to absolve my survivor's guilt before we left Glasgow, when she clutched my arm and said she wanted me to find a new partner. 'You deserve to be loved,' she said, and looked up with that slender smile. Yes, really: my dying wife, in her final months, wanted to ease the pain of living for me.

Easter was celebrated in the hospice with a lavish breakfast. The dining table was dominated by moulded chocolate eggs which my parents had brought from France to Glasgow, and whose odyssey was completed when I brought them back across the North Sea to be devoured in The Hague. In the afternoon I would fly out to Glasgow to finish packing the house. When I returned five days later it would be as an immigrant.

'I'm getting stronger every day,' Magteld said. It became her mantra. By the time I first saw her in The Hague she had dispensed with the disability cutlery and reverted to regular utensils. Above her bed hung her gym, a hard plastic triangle with a rubber band stretched round it. She showed me how she used it to pull herself up, gritting her teeth as she urged her failing arms to raise her from the divan. Within a few days she was able to wheel herself across the vinyl floors. Her breathing became deeper, her voice richer,

her expression less strained. One night, as we lay in bed talking softly, she laughed so hard that one of the nurses rushed upstairs in alarm.

I kissed her goodbye after lunch. I wasn't worried, this time, about not seeing her again. She would be there on Friday, and the next week we were seeing an oncologist about a new course of treatment. The fear had ebbed.

On the way to the airport I checked in on the house, where a delegation from the family was working like bees to decorate the empty bedrooms. Magteld had chosen the colours herself, wheeling herself round the wide aisles of the DIY store, concentration etched in the lines of her face. The builders were rapidly installing new back doors and two bathrooms. Metal ramps were attached to the thresholds so Magteld could move about the ground floor. One day, I hoped, we would carry her up the stairs to see the children's new rooms.

In Glasgow I bought a new pair of trousers and a jacket as I assumed the role of the émigré. Two removal men arrived on Wednesday night and reduced the house to a shell in a few hours. The van left in the morning to catch the overnight ferry from Hull. On the final Friday I had lunch with my parents in the Babbity Bowster pub, a ritual that had begun two decades earlier on one of my first visits to the city.

I boarded the train at Central Station, bound for Edinburgh airport and Amsterdam. The sky was dark violet, as if a storm was ushering me out of the country. At Schiphol airport I was waved through the border without a whiff of ceremony. It could hardly be further removed from the jubilant arrival Magteld and I had imagined for years. Everything was drably familiar: the baggage carousel, the black-walled basement station and the yellow trains, the glass and concrete palace of Den Haag Centraal. Only when I reached the hospice and took Magteld in my arms again did I feel a stir of accomplishment.

On Monday morning I took the boys to the town hall to register as residents. Magteld had already registered, using the hospice as her home address. I packed our passports and the sales contract for the house and boarded the tram to the centre of The Hague. We sat down opposite a courteous, unsmiling young woman, and I set out the paperwork.

'Is their mother not with you?' she asked.

'She's here, but she's in a hospice,' I replied. 'She's too sick to travel here.'

I gave her Magteld's name and the address of the hospice, emphasising she was a Dutch national. The woman scrolled through her screen and ruffled the papers on the table a few times, accompanied by increasingly vigorous shakes of the head. There was no record.

'If she's moved here from abroad she needs to register in person,' she told me.

'But she's in a hospice . . .' I began.

'What is that, a hospice?'

I hesitated. Had my pronunciation let me down? Was there a different Dutch word I was meant to use? Or were hospices simply beyond the scope of this woman's experience?

'Well, she's seriously ill . . .'

Her eyes narrowed. 'Was there a medical reason for you wanting to move here?' she asked.

'No,' I said with a tingle of irritation. 'That came later.'

But she was unwavering: the rules were the rules and there were no exceptions. New migrants, including returning Dutch citizens, were required to present themselves in person. She handed us our residency papers and made an appointment for us to return with Magteld, in two weeks' time.

A week later a typed letter arrived from the mayor, Jozias van Aartsen, in English, welcoming us to his city. It began: 'I am delighted that you have come to live here and I hope you will soon feel at home' and came with a free voucher for the library. The underlying message didn't escape me, however, and the following week the first municipal tax demand duly landed on the doormat.

The folder containing Magteld's medical history squatted on her desk in the hospice. Most of its pages were devoted to the last eighteen months. We gathered it up and took it down to the hospital, where Dr Barrett had arranged an appointment with an oncologist.

The first hurdle was getting past reception. The receptionist needed to see proof of Magteld's insurance cover before giving her clearance. But she was only eligible for health insurance once she had registered as a resident, and that had been stalled for another two weeks. There was a nervous stand-off for a few moments, the irresistible force of Magteld's cancer grinding against the immovable object of Dutch bureaucracy, until I remembered the European health cards in my wallet. For the time being she would have to be treated as a tourist.

After a short wait we were shown into a narrow side room and introduced to a cancer surgeon who had thumbed through Magteld's dossier. 'The last few years haven't been a very happy story,' he said soberly. He put us through to his colleagues in the oncology department. I got a phone call the next day and a week later Magteld had an appointment.

The HagaZiekenhuis was a high monolithic building whose pristine corridors echoed with the rippling sound of staff bustling about in white rubber clogs. Magteld's new oncologist emerged from a consultation room and shook both our hands. Dr Houtsma was an earnest, softly spoken man with wiry hair, his face steeped in kindness and compassion. He set out the facts of Magteld's case diligently and without panic. But neither did he shy from the fact that her disease was at a very advanced stage.

Magteld sat with a small blue notebook in her trembling hand, containing the notes she had scrawled in the hospice. In a year and a half she had gained some fluency in the language of cancer medicine. She discussed the options with Dr Houtsma in the unhurried tone that she had cultivated in meetings with council officials and politicians. Was paciltaxel or carboplatin a better option, she wanted to know. She was taking dexamethasone to contain the inflammation in her lungs, but the side-effects were severe and would soon start to erode her liver, so the dose would need to be scaled back. Dr Houtsma told her to prepare herself for a new course of chemotherapy. A final roll of the dice.

Before deciding how to proceed, he needed Magteld to undergo a scan to establish the extent of her cancer. There was no need to worry about delays: the scan was already booked for the next day. Then he turned to me and asked, 'And how are things with you?'

I jolted in my seat. I was accustomed to being the supporting act or the invisible stagehand in these consultations, but here was a medical professional breaking through the fourth wall.

'Um, well, it's pretty hard going,' I murmured.

'It's extremely hard,' he corrected me. He had listened attentively to the story of our migration, the speed of Magteld's decline and the challenges we faced resettling the children. He made a second appointment with the social care department, to see what support we were entitled to as a family.

By the time we emerged from the consultation room, having shaken hands a second time with Dr Houtsma, the day seemed appreciably brighter. A proper plan would have to wait, however, until after the weekend. More appointments were scheduled over the next few days. There seemed to be an endless stream of specialists lining up to take their turn at treating Magteld, like dancers in a ballroom. A physiotherapy team warned us to check our medical insurance covered all the various treatments Magteld would be undergoing. 'If you start doing supervised sports the costs can rack up quickly,' one said.

I looked at her in her wheelchair, and she looked back at me, lightly shocked. Were they really talking about Magteld getting up and not just walking but playing sport?

For the boys and me the beach house would be our base for the next two weeks. It was one of hundreds of large brick chalets laid out behind the dunes at the southern end of the city. Gaunt, wispy trees poked out of the arid soil which, when the wind scampered in from the shore, gave it an end-of-the-world feel.

Magteld's parents and I went for walks on the beach or sat on the small patio drinking coffee while the boys roamed through the woods and fetched sticks which Adam arranged, diligently, on the threshold. We headed into the city to see Magteld at the hospice, or I took her out for lunch or coffee. Sometimes I would bring her back to the beach house and we would have tea together, in a strange parody of a family weekend break. It was mainly a matter of eating up the time until she could start her medical treatment again.

Soldiers remembering a war speak of moments of terror interspersed by spells of unbearable tedium. The waiting, sometimes, could be suffocating. One afternoon at the beach house I went out to the scrub of lawn where Magteld was sitting in her chair, wrapped tightly in a shawl, a soft breeze flicking her hair. Her eyes were half-closed and her mouth, I saw as I moved closer, was clenched in a grimace. She was exhausted and on the verge of tears.

'Gordon,' she croaked, 'take me back to the hospice.'

'What's wrong?' I asked.

'Just take me back.'

In the car she told me she had wheeled herself outside to escape the suppressed tension in the house. Her mother had followed her out and asked if she was having a bad day. It had shredded the last remnants of her patience. There were too few days already; Magteld no longer had the luxury of wasting one. She had wanted a brief moment alone, to recover her strength and banish the creeping fear. There was a bad day coming, and she wasn't ready to face it yet.

10

The last weeks of Magteld's life were a time of tremendous hope. I never want to forget that, however contradictory it sounds. We talked of trips to the beach and drinking prosecco at sundown. She found an article in the local freesheet about *Vlaggetjesdag*, when the first catch of the herring season is ceremonially landed at Scheveningen harbour, and magnet-pinned it to the fridge. Daytrippers fill the quaysides and flock round the dozen stalls serving up that unmistakably Dutch delicacy of raw herring sprinkled with onions and clapped in a white bun. That was in mid-June, six weeks away. Soon after that it would be the school holidays. Perhaps by then she would be well enough to enjoy a short trip away. We even concocted a fanciful scheme to hire a campervan and charge down to Lake Garda, where our story had begun twenty-one years earlier.

'Dr Barrett wasn't right, then,' Diny said one evening over a glass of wine. I thought of Magteld's story of the man with the newspaper and shrugged. The truth was nobody knew how long Magteld had left. All we could do was keep filling up the days.

The hospice was meant to be a final staging post – in its own words, a 'near-home', with everything that implied. Sometimes, however, the guests thrived so well under the round-the-clock care that their condition stabilised and they were able to leave. Magteld's desire to spend her remaining time with her family, in the house she had found for us, would not be quashed, and she quietly began making arrangements to be discharged. Only later did it become clear how tenaciously she clung to her wish to die at home, in her own bed, with her three boys by her side.

The house was a jungle of boxes and building materials, the staircase draped in dust sheets and the bed buried under an avalanche of clothes and linen. The noise of drills and hammers tore through the air. The boys' bedrooms would not be ready for another week, so Luc and Diny took them away for five days to Sleen, the closest thing they had to a family home.

I went on shuttle runs to the local branch of Ikea, in Delft. Nothing illustrated my transition from tourist to resident better than the fact that I mainly associated Johannes Vermeer's hometown with self-assembly furniture. Magteld had marked the catalogue on her iPad, picking out table lamps and a picnic table set for the garden. Together with Sanneke I unpacked the kitchen, which had taken me days to decant into boxes, in a whirling few hours. In the evenings I sat, alone, screwing together chipboard panels to the point of exhaustion. Gradually the pile of boxes dwindled, the builders retreated and a home emerged from the clutter. By the end of April I was able to move in.

I saw Magteld in the hospice once or twice a day, scheduling my visits to work around her afternoon naps. I fetched her from her room, performing the well-oiled transition from bed to wheelchair, and followed her as she rolled herself into the lift. Her eyes glinted as she scrambled with her fingertips to gain purchase on my arms when I transferred her to the chair, and again when I reached down to steal a kiss.

She had arranged to spend the next Saturday night in the house. If it went well, I thought, she could divide her time between home and hospice. I had metal ramps installed in the doorways and went out to a disability supply store to fetch a roller seat for the shower.

My parents visited later that week. For them the journey across the sea, from Harwich to Hook of Holland, was more convenient than the long drive to Glasgow. We had tea with Magteld, in the hospice, and I cooked supper in the house the next day. At the end of the meal I brought through a steaming jug of hot water, having forgotten to put the beans in the coffee filter. 'He's got a lot on his mind,' I heard Magteld say from the kitchen, and my parents chuckled. To be in her home, amusing herself with her family, surrounded by the chattels of her life in Scotland, was what she lived for now.

At the hospice the paperwork was piling up. Magteld worked in concentrated bursts, in between sleeps, declining offers of help from the staff and volunteers. Adam was due to begin school on 6 May, a Tuesday, since Monday was Liberation Day, when the Dutch celebrate the end of the wartime occupation. Euan needed a place at a special school, which was a more time-consuming affair. We had begun the process back in February by contacting schools and education authorities, and they replied with an avalanche of questionnaires to assess his capacity to learn, his social interaction, his hobbies, his communication skills and behavioural problems: Does he mostly play alone? Does he make inappropriate noises? Does he bite? Does he steal? Does he hear voices? Is he suicidal? We waited. Around six weeks later a letter arrived from a specialist school telling us we hadn't provided enough information.

We sat in our house and hacked our way through another bundle of questionnaires, including one we had already completed first time around. Magteld kept up the pressure: she made phone calls, followed up paperwork and made appointments, employing the doggedness she had learned on the parent council. And then she waited. Dutch bureaucracy moves like a windmill pulverising a pile of grist, but Magteld didn't have the luxury of patience.

One of her visitors in the hospice was Diana, a cancer patient she had befriended on the blogging grapevine. Diana had first been diagnosed with breast cancer around the time Magteld and I were married, nearly thirteen years earlier, and had had secondary cancer for the last five. Living for five years with an incurable disease might seem an unbearable burden, but Diana was indefatigable and inspiring. She immersed herself in the latest medical research, became conversant in the matrix of data that measured the progress of her tumours, and challenged her consultants without fear. She showed Magteld that a terminal diagnosis was far from a helpless situation, and that patients could play an active role in their treatment.

Social media gave Magteld a sense of solidarity with people who shared an unwanted fate. She got to know them not as patients but as people with jobs, partners, interests, children, political opinions and senses of humour. She loved to watch the replies to her blogs come in from all over the world, from friends and family, from vague acquaintances and people who only knew her as a jumble of pixels on a screen, yet could still connect with the woman who sat in her wheelchair typing, hundreds or thousands of miles away.

Five weeks had passed since Magteld and I last shared our bed in Glasgow. Seventeen stairs separated it from the ground floor, and she glided up and down them effortlessly until the day she was abruptly taken to hospital. Now a flight of stairs was an impenetrable barrier. In The Hague I had to wheel her into the bedroom, lift her from the chair onto the bed and pull her pyjamas on as if dressing an infant. Yet what a thrill it was to lie beside her on that Saturday night, even though she had to be handled as delicately as an ancient manuscript. She woke every few hours demanding painkillers, or a pear ice-cream to soothe her prickly throat, or *dropstaafjes* – hard little liquorice sweets – as a nostalgic comfort when the dread of the deep night came upon her. But just to feel the weight and warmth of her was worth every tribulation. In the morning we would have breakfast together, with Magteld at the head of the table, and I could kiss her forehead and drink in her weary smile, and it would vindicate the battles we fought on the journey to dawn.

We watched the constant stream of bicycles flow past the window, that classically Dutch symphony of style and function. Bikes customised with flowers, or with beads in the spokes, or plastic crates strapped to the front as makeshift shopping carriers. Mothers carrying children front and back, or towed along in covered trailers, or strapped into vast wooden tubs at the prow end. Bikes used to convey bathroom scrap, small dogs (large ones ran alongside), paintings, musical instruments, and desirable others who perched giggling on the shopper rack.

The beach was tantalisingly close – five minutes in the car, ten minutes at a fast jog – so I could run up to it in the mornings. We could leave the house at five o'clock on a summer's afternoon and spend a few hours at a beach shack, sipping coffee or wine as the children played in the sand and jumped in the waves beneath a reddening sun, before drifting home, fresh and recharged. The Hague makes few concessions to the conventions of seaside towns, with the exception of the promenade at Scheveningen, with its casinos, neon-fronted bars, ice-cream parlours and shops groaning with gaudy airbeds and bubble-text T-shirts.

Further down the coast the beach is separated from the city by the dunes, where the Dutch have tried to let nature take its course, but the pathways and regimented trees betray their instinct for the straight line. Send a group of Dutch children to the beach with buckets and spades and before long they'll be digging a canal.

We'd discussed euthanasia before leaving Scotland. It reassured Magteld to know that if her pain became unbearable, the Netherlands would allow her to end her life peacefully, with her doctor's consent and cooperation. At that stage she had nothing worse than a severe cough, but the knowledge that she could become acutely ill in a short time dogged her.

Euthanasia was a comfort, not a threat. I hated knowing she was dying and loathed the disease that was grinding her down, but it was worse still to see her writhe in pain. The most dreadful moments were deep in the night in Glasgow, when she leapt out of bed, screaming, 'Kill me now!' It would be a monstrous cruelty, I thought, to prolong a life when only suffering remained. And I remembered the colleague who developed an aggressive cancer at an even younger age and took his own life when he was told he had a matter of days left to live.

In her bedside cabinet at the hospice was an envelope containing a 'do not resuscitate' letter, one of the last documents she ever signed. Assisted dying was something she would have to discuss with her family doctor, once she had acquired one. That was another pressing reason to sort out her residency: she needed to be a resident to access insurance, and she needed to be insured before a doctor would take her on.

Among the other guests in the hospice was 'Robert', a garrulous man who seemed to be in his late forties. He had led an active life until he was confined to his bed by paraplegia, and now had to be wheeled down, prostrate, in the lift for mealtimes, where he held court from his elevated position. He talked freely and openly, seemingly in no pain. We never saw him receive visitors. For all the strong sense of camaraderie, the residents sometimes grated on each other, and Magteld sometimes flashed her eyes and muttered at me not to encourage him.

When my parents came for lunch Robert told some of his life story: he had left the Netherlands as a young man, with a basic schooling, and worked as a barman in more than twenty countries around the world. He was proud of his achievements and his workmanlike English, gleaned from his days on the road. Of his own nation he was enthusiastic: 'This is the best country to live in the world. There's always someone to look after you.'

I became fond of him when he told Magteld she was lucky to have a strong man looking after her, even though I often felt ready to break in those days. On the Friday before her weekend at home Magteld shared some unexpected news. 'Robert's going home,' she said. Her eyes were bright, and I saw she was excited, both for his sake and for her own.

'Who's going to look after him?' I said.

'A friend of his is taking him in. He doesn't have long. He's just going to enjoy his last days. Isn't it great?'

I could see her reasoning: if bed-bound Robert could spend his final days at home, surely she could, too.

I took her back to the hospice on Sunday morning. It was *Dodenherdenking* – Remembrance Day, the eve of the liberation celebrations – and tricolour flags at half mast were draped over the city in memory of the war dead. The lift was out of order, so a bed was made up for Magteld in the office downstairs. I went into the dining room so she could rest and the boys could play with the giant teddy bears. Robert was there, in his bed, dressed for his grand departure in a clean shirt and trousers.

Two ambulance personnel walked in and rigged up a mobile stretcher next to his bed so they could carry him out of the door. But Robert's spine was too brittle for them to risk manhandling him. The only way he could escape the divan was to raise himself up on the triangular hook that dangled above him, so they could swing his legs across and lower him down.

Robert looked to the left. It was a distance of no more than three feet, but to him it must have looked like a ravine. He puffed his cheeks out and forced a few stiff breaths from his shallow lungs. His eyes focused on the ring, and he gripped it tightly with his fingers. Then, with a hoarse scream, he summoned all his strength, raised himself off the bed and dragged himself over to the stretcher, where he lay catching his breath and smiling weakly but triumphantly. A candle was lit in the lobby, and a song was played to accompany him out. The last I heard as the doors closed was his voice trailing away as he was pushed into the sunlight and the fresh air. Then the engine of the ambulance roared, and he was gone.

Magteld came back home on Monday night. Adam was starting school the next day, and she wanted to be there on his first morning. When I fetched her from the hospice in the afternoon I saw immediately her head was down, and in a muted voice she told me about Robert.

'He didn't go home,' she said. 'He had an appointment with his doctor. He died yesterday. He'd arranged euthanasia.'

The story about a friend looking after him had been a fictional vignette. I thought back to that moment the day before, when he had raised himself from his bed. How he had grimaced and used every ounce of strength left in his wasted body to cross the gap to the stretcher. Had he been anything less than one hundred per cent certain of his intention, had his resolve wavered even for a second, I felt sure he would not have managed it. His will to die was absolute and unbending. He had called me a 'strong man' and told Magteld not to worry about the children's future, and that was a fine sentiment, but I'm not sure I will ever have the strength, physical or mental, to commit myself to my own demise as he did.

Magteld, however, was having second thoughts. She had too much to do in life. She kept the 'do not resuscitate' directive, but never mentioned euthanasia again.

On Monday night, as Magteld lay in our bed, I sat up sharpening pencils and preparing Adam's schoolbag for the next day. The next stage of our journey was the 500-yard walk to the school gates. For Adam it was a dive into a vortex. His life had been wrenched from its foundations as if by a hurricane. And now he was being sent to a strange school where everyone spoke in a language that was still largely foreign to him.

His anxiety took the form of a wordless anger and an ironclad refusal to comply with the most basic instruction. He needed stability, reassurance and warmth. But his mother was dying, and both of us were hamstrung by grief and apprehension. Two days before school I lost my temper with him, and in his frustration he propelled himself head-first into the glass of the sliding doors between the two main rooms. Fortunately it left him with nothing worse than a cut nose. It earned me a tart rebuke from Magteld: 'I missed the adult in that relationship,' she said.

I was unable to provide the comfort he needed. I was terrified of losing Magteld, of failing to adapt to her country, of Euan and Adam condemning me for taking them on the whole senseless escapade. As long as she lived, Magteld dominated our perspective like a setting winter sun.

The next morning we set off for school, the boys racing ahead on their scooters as I pushed Magteld along. In the first few days I mastered the contours of the neighbourhood: the loose paving stones, dropped kerbs, manhole covers, tree roots and concealed gutters, every dip and bevel. The headmaster came out from the school to greet us, together with Adam's class teacher. He had gym on the first day, which we hoped would be a welcome distraction. For five minutes we stood and chatted around Magteld in her wheelchair, like hikers pausing at the top of a hill to enjoy the view. And then we took Euan home, to resume a domestic life that was threatening to become orderly.

11

Dr Houtsma was cautiously enthusiastic when we saw him again the following Monday. He summarised the results of the scan. There was no way to sanitise the fact that Magteld's cancer had spread further. A new cluster of cells was putting her hip under strain, which explained why she had been struggling to swing her legs out of bed for the last few mornings.

Dr Houtsma looked up and paused a beat. 'Do you want to see the scan?' he asked.

Magteld looked uneasy. Dr Houtsma sat perfectly still. He seemed ready to wait all afternoon. The smile never left his face. And then Magteld said, 'Yes.'

It was like watching a grotesque game show. He turned the screen towards Magteld to reveal an image of her skeleton. Most of the picture was a faint grey, but her spine was a shocking strip of white. 'Anything white is a concern,' he explained. We looked again, this time in faint horror.

Magteld's backbone was as shrill as a neon sign. She looked at me uneasily, her upper teeth clenching her lower lip. The only grey area in the entire length of her backbone was the patch just below her shoulders which had been targeted by the radiotherapy just before she left Glasgow. And even there the cancer cells were starting to regroup.

There were a few shreds of hope. The lesions in Magteld's right lung had shrunk, though on the opposite side they had become tumours. A bigger complication was her hip, which was at risk of breaking. Because of this Dr Houtsma decided on a short course of radiotherapy, followed by a new course of chemotherapy, comprising six sessions of paciltaxel and carboplatin. She would lose her hair again and could expect more gruelling side effects. And, though he didn't spell it out, it would probably give her a few months at most. It was a high price, but perhaps we could steal one last summer.

'I'll go for it if you will,' Dr Houtsma said.

'Absolutely,' said Magteld.

But the radiotherapist, whom we saw next, took a different view. Stabilising Magteld's hip for the duration of her chemotherapy would require around ten treatment sessions. The chemotherapy would need to be put back a further week to 28 May. We agreed: what difference would a week make at this stage? Magteld was getting stronger every day, after all, and the prize of regaining movement in her hip, perhaps even ditching the wheelchair, was worth waiting for.

We came away with a printout of radiotherapy dates, all at different times of day, so I would have to manage Adam's school times around them. Back home I pulled out the diary and tried to untangle the logistical knots of the next two weeks.

A phone call from the hospice that afternoon brought a cold shock. It was one of the managers, asking if I had all the home-care arrangements set up. 'No,' I replied, a little bemused.

'I need to know that you've got everything arranged,' she explained. 'Magteld's being discharged tomorrow.'

Behind the scenes Magteld had been plotting her exit. Most of the practical issues had been anticipated. A nurse would come to the house for an hour every morning, to help her out of bed, shower her and get her dressed. I just had to take care of the rest: shopping, cooking, helping her get about, the school run. 'It'll be fine,' Magteld said when I spoke to her. The tinge of irritation in her voice snuffed out any nascent objection I might have had.

Once my panic receded I had to pause and applaud her tenacity. She had it all worked out.

I arrived at the hospice on Tuesday morning and filled two suitcases with her clothes and toiletries, as if she were returning from holiday. She was bright and cheerful, and the volunteers formed a guard of honour as I wheeled her through the front door. There was no fanfare, no parting song, no candle burning in the hallway. This was a home-coming, the conclusion of an odyssey.

Our fragmented lives coalesced into a routine, a buttress of domesticity against the encroaching darkness. The days were tightly choreographed. I got up and fixed breakfast: a bowl of muesli for Magteld, laced with yoghurt and pieces of fruit; for Euan and Adam the familiar Dutch opener of bread topped with chocolate sprinkles, most of which cascaded onto the floor. I brought Magteld's iPad to the table so she could read while the boys got ready for school. We set off on the scooters, and by the time Euan and I returned, ten minutes or so later, the duty nurse had usually arrived. At weekends I ran to the beach while she was in the house, finding relief in the open sky and the cool, firm sand. There were three nurses, all women, working in rotation, and Magteld quickly struck up a rapport with each of them. They gave her a shower and counted out her pills into the little plastic boxes, marked for every day of the week. Then we sat and talked, about Magteld's upcoming appointments, how she was feeling, and, once that was done, about life, work, the weather and children.

On fine days we went for walks, up to the little square at the end of the street or to the supermarket. I flipped down the footrests in her wheelchair, slipped her shoes onto her feet and pulled her arms into her jacket, feeling the grim protrusions in her spine as I smoothed it against her back. Then she settled back into her wheelchair and we rolled over the ramps and out of the door, flanked by the boys. Sometimes Euan or Adam pushed the chair, in keeping with the doctors' advice that they would benefit from taking an active role in her care. They complied, but uncomfortably, and at junctions I took over to protect her back from the jutting kerbs.

We had lunch in the garden, a southwest-facing patio bordered by mature trees, which needed only a kiss of sunshine to feel pleasantly warm. Some days I would roll her down to the fish stall at the crossroads and treat us to a prawn salad, or *kroketten* with mustard, the original Dutch fast-food delicacy. After lunch she would nap until I fetched Adam from school, while Euan watched television or played with his Lego in his bedroom. At the weekend we went to a beach café with Sanneke and Sjoerd, savouring coffee and toast and the warm salty breeze while the children ran down to paddle in the lapping waves. In the evenings we sat in front of the television, like a regular family, Magteld watching *Masterchef* with the children while I cooked dinner.

One day Euan came downstairs and beckoned me up to his room. His Lego, which was usually scattered all over the floor, had been tidied away into the plastic containers. He laughed at my astonished reaction. And then I realised that his mother, confined to the ground floor, had still never been in his bedroom, so I fetched the iPad and filmed both the boys' bedrooms, so that Magteld could see what their new domains looked like.

The hospital's radiotherapy unit was in the basement, through a maze of corridors and double doors, past storage rooms stuffed with rubber tubing and alien devices. The last stage was an old lift accessed through two heavy swing doors, which could only be pushed open manually. It was an unlikely thing to encounter in a Dutch hospital, as if we had accidentally intruded on an old film set. If Euan and Adam were with us they took on the role of door attendants while I wheeled Magteld through. I left her with a pile of magazines, a book and Euan, who played quietly on the iPad or read as she sat in the treatment room, while I dashed to the shops or fetched Adam from school.

Nearly every minute of the day was timetabled: in between appointments I had to make time for cooking, cleaning, washing, shopping, and still let the boys out to play. Maintaining the illusion of normality was crucial. In this respect we were fortunate, since The Hague has a wealth of play-parks, most of them festooned with gleaming apparatus. Dutch cities sometimes look as if they were not so much designed as poured from a giant mould; as the old joke goes, God made the world, but the Dutch improved it.

Night was the most fraught time. Magteld wilted as darkness closed in but was often too restless to sleep. Sometimes she lay in bed, reading or trying to settle into her pillows, while I sat in the dining room with a book, or on the computer, or just stepped back for a moment from the whirl of the day. Sometimes, in the murky realm between wakefulness and sleep, panic would take hold, and I would shuffle wearily into the bedroom to calm her.

The first night after she came home was exhausting. Every hour or so she cried out for painkillers, or a pear ice-cream, or sweets, or more medicine and usually another ice-cream. Every time I lurched out of bed I felt like a sodden towel being retrieved from a toilet bowl. An hour's unbroken sleep was a rare treasure. As day broke, it brought a new cycle of chores, and I had to scrape together the energy to make breakfast, transport Magteld from bedroom to dining table to toilet to sofa to car, do the housework and keep the boys occupied. I had the sleep pattern of a new father, with none of the euphoria. It might go on for several months yet. But the fear of it stopping was even worse.

Fatigue was seeping back into our lives like a river that has burst its banks. At some point during one of those early nights I turned to her and confessed I wasn't sure if I could cope with it.

She gritted her teeth and half closed her eyes. A molten core of anger rose in her voice. 'Don't you dare say that,' she seethed.

'I'm just being honest,' I said.

I was shocked to see she was crying. As I tried to explain she became more distressed. She began hitting me, frenziedly. I felt the sting of her fingers as her limp fists slapped against my chest. 'Just don't send me back to the hospice,' she croaked.

Those awful, impotent slaps made me feel wretched. Months later, when I spoke to one of the nurses who cared for her, she admitted candidly, 'She was strong, but she was a very sick woman.' For the first time I saw clearly why Magteld had been so determined to discharge herself from the hospice. She had decided, rationally and in full cognisance of the risks, that she would rather spend what time she had in her house, with the people she loved. She preferred a day in the sunlight to a week in the shade. What horror, what resolve, what courage. Little wonder, then, that when I threatened to desert her as she hovered on the rim of oblivion, she had lashed out. If I failed now, I would fail at love.

Over the next few nights I developed a routine. Before going to bed I set out a macabre buffet on her side table: paracetamol, a bottle of morphine, a small bowl loaded with her favourite sweets. She would try to get through the night on two pear ice-creams. My spells of sleep stretched from an hour to two, sometimes two and a half. It was tolerable, no more. Relief came with the glow of dawn, the hour of breakfast, and the arrival of the duty nurse to begin the next day's cycle.

For the epigraph to her memoir, *Love's Work*, the philosopher Gillian Rose chose a saying attributed to the Russian monk and saint Silouan the Athonite: 'Keep your mind in hell, and despair not.' *Love's Work* was written while Rose was dying of cancer and is an intense meditation on the meaning of life and love. It may seem puzzling at first glance for a modern academic to adopt the words of a barely literate ascetic. Silouan claimed most of his wisdom was received in visions from God during a life of unstinting prayer; Rose lived a life of studied eroticism, both in the primary sense and that of having an endless passion and curiosity for life. So what inspiration did this secular prophet of love draw from a man who dedicated his life to a private dialogue with his deity?

Rose talks at one stage about 'the unhappiness of one who refuses to dwell in hell, and who lives, therefore, in the most static despair'. The hell she refers to is a state of mind, the place where pain and suffering and mortal fear lurk. Dwelling in hell is the antithesis of the modern malaise of 'positive thinking'. It means not shutting out death or suffering, or believing it can be overcome through virtuous living, but accepting it as intrinsic to life. Christians interpret Silouan's words as an invocation to remain humble before God and submit to Jesus as your saviour, but Rose places them firmly in the secular realm. She quotes approvingly her oncologist when he says: 'I know there is no natural justice, because you, who have harmed no one, have cancer, while Saddam Hussein does not.' It is liberating to divorce death from notions of justice and glory, and accept it as the universal event that it is. It renders life meaningless and precious all at once. The value of a life is wholly determined by how it affects other living beings. Martyrdom and the death penalty are absurd notions, because they confer moral authority on an indiscriminate process. Nobody deserves to die, and yet everybody does.

In Magteld's last weeks we were consciously living in hell, but it was a hell that she had shaped and furnished, and that was oddly comforting. The sense of pain and discomfort was imprinted in every step; simple tasks such as tying shoelaces became aggravating trials. And all the time we knew that the trajectory of her demise could nosedive at any moment. Most people learn to cope with this process over decades, but for Magteld it was compressed into a few months.

One of the duty nurses told her, 'You don't have to live with pain.' It is a peculiar twenty-first-century conceit that medicine, by anaesthetising physical pain, can remove suffering. The novelist Haruki Murakami, in the very different context of his memoir on running, coined the epigram: 'Pain is inevitable, suffering is optional'. As a runner this appeals to me, but in other aspects of life it falls short. Suffering is not always avoidable; the real choice is whether or not to despair. Magteld was constantly confronted by her impending extinction. It was present in every twinge of her back, every cough, every faltering step and clean-and-jerk lift between the bed and the wheelchair. Yet she rarely despaired. In dying she had learned how to live, but only once she had learned to temper her suffering by cultivating her own corner of hell.

She had the freedom to dismiss the banal injustices of traffic jams and supermarket queues and slow internet connections, and concentrate instead on what was worthwhile and beautiful. But while Magteld cherished every hour we spent together as a family, I had to consider the life to come, alone with the children, while simultaneously trying not to think about it. Our world was contained in a sealed glass box on the surface of a lifeless planet. Magteld's physical realm had shrunk to an area of a few square miles, defined by the beach at one end and the hospital at the other, yet as long as the box remained intact we could still pretend life was carrying on as normal.

Sometimes the illusion flickered. We were in the bathroom one evening, brushing her teeth before she went to bed. There wasn't enough space for Magteld and her wheelchair in the room, so I had to lift her out and twist myself out of the way while she balanced in my arms. What were a few small steps for other people had become a precarious spacewalk. She leaned on the sink and brushed feverishly, keening for the firmness of the chair. When she was finished I steered her backwards into the chair, but this time her leg buckled and she slumped to the floor. She lay crumpled on the tiles, shunting out the breaths, her face a mask of startled terror. We had become old without warning, frail and fearful. I still had the body of a healthy person in the twilight of youth, and so, but for a few decisive aberrations, did she. But in that moment we saw a lucid apparition of the fate that awaited us, as ghastly as a fetid swamp. I could read her thoughts: *When did I become this limp bundle of rags? How much worse is this going to get?*

With a tremendous effort I lifted her off the floor, and put her in the chair, and kissed her on the forehead, and she gave me that soft, tight-lipped, fearful smile, and we staggered into bed to gather strength for the next day.

Was it really a privilege to survive? Magteld would die soon, surrounded by her family and those who loved her, warmed by their hands and moistened by their tears as she vanished into eternity. She would live on in our memories, in shared anecdotes, a reassuring presence, like a monument, ever young, ever beautiful, her imperfections smoothed by time and softened by the mist of memory. I had to stagger on, raise her children in the shadow of her absence, the core of my soul gnawed away by her cancer. Was it really better to give up one's last breaths half a century later, alone, withered and forgotten, in the amnesic surroundings of institution-alised care?

The boys would be Scottish expats rather than semi-natives. Ghosts and echoes would linger in Magteld's house, occupy our dining table, our sofa and our bed. The absence of her laugh ringing in the hallway, her non-footsteps creaking on the stairs. She understood the looming hell better than I did. The dead are taken care of; it's the living who need looking after.

The day after she moved in I took Magteld to register at the council office. The town hall resembled a giant futuristic church, with a huge open atrium where the citizens were processed, while above their heads officials bustled about on open walkways over ten storeys, their silhouettes filtering the light like stained-glass saints. It was appropriate for what was essentially a confirmation ritual that would also, mercifully, resolve the opaque status of her medical insurance cover.

The appointment was scheduled for 9.20 a.m. I arranged for the support nurse to arrive half an hour earlier so I could take Adam to school, pick up Magteld from the house and wheel her down to the tram stop. She packed two vials of morphine in case her spine flared up, selected her best jacket, and we set off down the road. Fate allocated us a tram driver who flung the vehicle around every corner as if test-driving a rollercoaster. By the time we arrived in the city centre twenty minutes later Magteld's face was stretched in pain and she had polished off both morphine vials.

The Hague's streets were undergoing a facelift, with duckboards for pavements, streets closed off, cyclists weaving between pedestrians, and giant cranes performing surgery on lacerated buildings. For a wheelchair user it was an uncomfortable obstacle course, especially when at the mercy of an inexperienced helmsman. Somehow, despite doubling back at a couple of dead ends and taking a detour through a department store, we made it to the town hall only fifteen minutes after our allocated time.

I pulled a ticket from the machine and a few minutes later we were summoned to the front desk, me still slightly breathless and Magteld weary from battling the pain. A woman with ink-black hair cropped like a privet hedge greeted us without smiling. She sat on a raised platform, so our eyes were directly level; Magteld sat with her head below the desk, out of sight.

I gave our names. The woman peered at her computer screen, looked up again and shook her head. There was no record of us in the system.

I gave her the time and name of the appointment. She looked at the screen. Then looked at the clock over her left shoulder. Then looked back at me.

'Your appointment was at nine twenty,' she said. It was 9.40.

'I know,' I replied tersely.

'You need to be here on time, sir.'

We had been expunged, it seemed. I mumbled an excuse about being held up on the way. From down in her wheelchair Magteld grimaced and asked what the problem was.

The woman responded with a look that could have melted steel. 'We'll have to make a new appointment for you,' she said.

I looked down at Magteld. I looked back up at the woman and met her unflinching stare. I explained to her, in my plainest Dutch, that we would not be making another appointment. That I had wheeled Magteld to the town hall across an urban desert, in defiance of her pain. That we were here to sign her up as a resident in this, the international city of peace and justice. And that we were not going home until that task was complete.

The woman pressed a button on her computer. It spat out a paper ticket which she flung in my direction. 'Take this and join the first queue on the left. I don't know if or when they'll be able to help you.' She dismissed us with a turn of her head.

Where in this city, I wondered, would our autistic children learn about empathy?

I grabbed the ticket, uttered a curt thank-you to the side of her head and wheeled Magteld over to the queue. We waited less than five minutes. A polite young man called us over and checked the records on his computer.

'You're already registered in the system,' he said. 'Are you still living at the Jacobshospice?'

It turned out that the council had, after all, approved her application from the hospice. We breathed a sigh of bewildered relief, too exhausted for anger. All we had to do was register Magteld's new address.

'Can you do that for us?' I asked the man.

He shook his head. 'No. You'll have to take another ticket and go to that desk over there.' He gave a slightly apologetic smile as he explained this, the first sign of human warmth we had witnessed in this building. I wondered if he'd be reprimanded for it.

We waited another hour, and at the end of it the council records declared that Magteld and I were living together in the house she had chosen. We stopped at the supermarket and bought a box of ice lollies, one of which we shared as we rumbled along the duckboards back to the tram station. Thankfully, the journey back home was a good deal gentler and Magteld's pain had subsided. I wheeled her in through the door of what was now, officially, her home.

12

She was a devotee of TV drama, beginning with *Our Friends in the North* and graduating to *The Wire*, *The Killing*, *The Bridge*, *Wallander*. As housebound parents, we spent our evenings burning through boxsets. In the autumn before we left Glasgow we started on *Breaking Bad*. It might seem an odd choice for someone who had just gone through cancer treatment, but Magteld was quickly drawn in. It was, perhaps, a way of escaping the drama in our own lives to watch it as detached observers, in the fictional realm and on a more helter-skelter trajectory.

She considered writing a blog about Walter White's Icarus-like rise and fall. I saw parallels between the disease and White's personal development: he starts out producing crystal meth on a small scale, to provide for his family, but gradually the respectable chemistry teacher with a sideline metamorphoses into a ruthless drugs baron who permeates the supply chain. What begins as a minor deviation from a settled, unexceptional life metastasises and ravages every aspect of Walter White's life. You could say he becomes the cancer. It is an entropic process of chaos eclipsing order.

Perhaps Magteld was drawn in by White's well-meaning but ultimately ruinous desire to leave a legacy for his family. Or maybe she just enjoyed a gripping TV drama. When we reached the end of Season Four she shook her fist in triumph at the denouement. Sjoerd had disclosed the ending to her a few weeks earlier, while I was in Glasgow, and she had stubbornly kept it secret. I wondered if the fist-pump was a show of resistance, that she had survived to see the climax of her favourite show, like Simeon's bargain with God to glimpse the infant Jesus before departing this world.

The next day I ordered the final season from Amazon, so we could look forward to watching it the following week.

One of the tasks that occupied Magteld in the hospice was to find someone who could look after the boys during the week. If I could delegate part of the responsibility of child-care it would free up enough time to allow me to start looking for work (I'd been turned down for the job in Utrecht after the second interview). A short trail of phone calls led to Stephanie, who had worked with autistic children in Africa and was a trained music therapist. Magteld researched suitable interview questions and invited her to come to the house during our first weekend there. Over a cup of tea, accompanied by strawberry cream biscuits which I had bought in a misguided attempt to make the occasion more authentically

Dutch, and which remained untouched on the plate, we agreed she would start work nine days later, on a Tuesday.

Magteld posted an update on the progress of her radio-therapy on Facebook: 'So far I [have] had 3 and already feel the benefit . . . This weekend is lovely and we enjoy the sunshine at the beach. Tomorrow we go for it again.'

The Saturday was Euan's birthday. We had taken the tram into the city to buy a Lego set, ordered a cake from the local patisserie and invited the family to come and celebrate in the garden. In the few days beforehand Magteld had been struggling to settle at night, and her breathing was becoming heavier. Eight sessions of radiotherapy in ten days had drained her energy; there was one more on Monday, before chemotherapy began the next day.

She worried she would let Euan down by being too sick or too exhausted to make his eleventh birthday, and his first in The Hague, a memorable one.

'You'll be there for him,' I said. 'That's all he wants.'

Saturday was a bright, warm day. We sat in the sunshine demolishing creamy, softly crumbling millefeuilles topped with fruit, the standard-issue Dutch birthday cake. I was gently reproached for not providing the miniature forks that every Dutch household is supposed to keep for such occasions. Soft laughter rang through the house and wrapping paper piled up on the table as Euan tore open his presents. It was a scene Magteld must have visualised when she viewed the house in February. Next week would be June, the days were lengthening, and we looked forward to convening again over the summer.

The day before Euan's birthday Magteld had written her first blog in weeks, about the challenge of starting chemotherapy again. 'I will be losing my hair again and I could be ill for a few days and need rest.'

She asked me to edit and post it over the weekend. She liked to sit at her iPad and watch the web statistics page light up as readers all over the world connected with her.

Sunday morning was a precious moment of calm. Magteld had fought for breath in the night, and both of us were tired from the week's exertions. In the afternoon she rallied, and we decided to go outside, if only briefly, to feel the warmth of the sun and let the boys expend some energy.

We found a school playground where the gates were open. Magteld sat beneath a tree, to protect her irradiated skin from the sun. She didn't relish the potential irony of surviving one form of cancer only to be torpedoed by another. The boys scooted about the playground, which was laid out like a road network, dutifully following the roundabouts and dotted lines. The shadows of the leaves danced on her face as she watched the children following the markings on the ground.

So began the last twenty-four hours of Magteld's life.

Back home her breathing became more laboured. I asked if she wanted to go to hospital, but she declined. We were due there anyway in the morning for her final radiotherapy. I cooked *speklapjes* – long thick strips of bacon, one of many Dutch staples with which she had been reacquainting herself – with potatoes and broccoli. I surprised her with her favourite childhood dessert of steamed pears, having stumbled across them in the supermarket. Her eyes gleamed with nostalgic joy, and for a few minutes she sat looking at them as they sat on the table, swaddled in their own juices. I'd neglected to post her blog, and she had been annoyed at me, but the pears won her over. 'I'll do it in the morning,' I promised her, and kissed her tired cheeks.

Since we were waiting for the final series of *Breaking Bad* to arrive, we picked *Airplane* off the DVD shelf and watched it with the boys as the sun dimmed. I got the boys ready for bed first, followed by Magteld. I stayed up for a while, trying to write despite the enveloping fug of tiredness. A plaintive call from the bedroom shook me from my musings as I realised, with a pang of shame, that I was shutting out something greater than sleep. I lay with Magteld for a while to settle her, administering the trusted medicines of morphine, liquorice sweets and pear ice-cream. Her chest was rattling like a broken radiator.

'I don't mind if you take me to hospital tonight,' she muttered.

Soon afterwards her pain seemed to ease, her breathing became regular and she slipped into something like sleep, though I could feel how the struggle for breath cramped her whole body. At around midnight she asked me to lift her out of bed and wheel her to the dining-room table, because she couldn't rest lying down. She propped herself up on her elbows, took another ice-cream and tried to doze off. In the morning the nurse would come, and I would take Adam to school, and the resumption of our daily routine would bring relief.

After three hours of fitful sleep she called out again, in a soft, pained voice. I went through and sat with her. There was no doubt now that she had to go to hospital. I called the emergency line, described her symptoms and asked if she could be taken in.

She cut in, resisting. 'I don't want to go to hospital,' she snapped wheezily. 'I just want to know how I can breathe better.' How often must this scene have visited her in her darkest nightmares: the ambulance drawing up outside, two men removing her from the house, and the doors of the vehicle closing on her? Reluctant as I was to overrule her, I could see she was wilting fast.

The ambulance was dispatched. The woman on the line said it was not a blue-light call, meaning it would have to stop for red lights. It would be with us in about fifteen minutes.

After I put down the phone we sat together at the table, our hands entwined. We stroked each other's fingers gently and looked in each other's eyes. Neither of us said a word. The boys slept on upstairs, oblivious. Pallid light slowly filled the room.

The doorbell rang. An ambulance man of supernatural size filled the gloomy doorway. I led him through, followed by a smaller colleague, and they pulled up chairs at the dining-room table. In their unhurried Dutch manner, they asked Magteld to talk them through the events that had brought them to our door. The larger man's hands were like scoops. They listened both to her words and to the rasping grind of her lungs.

'You're all blocked up,' said the bigger man.

Magteld nodded. She no longer resisted. If anything, she looked relieved that the decision had been taken for her.

His hulking hands grabbed the handles of her wheelchair, and the pair of them pushed her out into the street, lifting her into the back of the ambulance as if she weighed no more than a blanket, and shut the doors.

'Are you coming with us?' said the smaller man.

I had barely slept, and I wanted to keep the children's routines as unblemished as possible. I would need to serve breakfast in a few hours. I said no. The ambulance man said nothing, but he held my gaze a few seconds longer than was comfortable.

The ambulance sped off down the road, its blue lights flashing and sirens wailing. I felt a sensation in my stomach as if I'd swallowed a hot chunk of lava.

I've no idea how I slept, but when the alarm went off two hours later I got up, made the children's breakfast and phoned the hospital. The doctor on duty told me Magteld had been given oxygen and antibiotics and was stable, but urged me to join her as soon as possible.

'What about her radiotherapy appointment?' I asked.

'She's in no condition to have that right now,' said the doctor. 'Do you have children?' she asked.

'Yes,' I said.

'Think about bringing them with you. I can't guarantee she'll survive this.'

I sent distress flares by text message to her parents and sisters. In a few minutes I would call Euan and Adam downstairs and explain to them, as they ate their sandwiches, why their mother was not there. I still wanted to send Adam to school, to preserve the sense of normality. If things took a turn for the worse he was only ten minutes away. Euan would have to come with me, since he had nowhere else to be.

Reality was breaking up. How could Magteld, who had been sitting in our garden toasting Euan's birthday less than forty-eight hours ago, now be lying in a hospital bed, rigged up to an oxygen mask and in mortal danger?

Because she had been in hospital in Glasgow recently she was deemed to pose a high risk of spreading foreign infections. We took the lift to the fifteenth floor and found her in an isolation room, separated from the corridor by a plastic curtain and covered in signs instructing all visitors to disinfect their hands. She was effectively quarantined.

She lay propped up by two pillows with a plastic mask on her face, her eyes bright, her breathing heavy and urgent. She gave me a smile and a little wave. The doctor came in a few minutes later. Magteld's eyes moistened as she looked at me and Euan while the doctor explained her situation. Her lungs were full of fluid, and the only way to clear them was to purge her system with oxygen. In her weakened, sleep-deprived state it was a far from risk-free exercise, but it was the only option. I understood it all with sudden, violent clarity.

And yet even now Magteld seemed fiercely, defiantly alive. I clutched her hand. After her secondary diagnosis in January I had promised to write her a poem, but I'd completely failed to even start on it. 'Don't go away,' I said. 'I'm going to write it for you.' She jerked her head up and down and smiled again.

A nurse came in and asked her how she was feeling. 'Better,' rasped Magteld. 'You don't have to say anything,' said the nurse. 'Save your energy.' She started explaining how she could offer Magteld an energising reiki massage, but Magteld cut her short with a vigorous shake of the head.

Dr Houtsma arrived a short time later. He was as frank and compassionate as ever, but his jaw was clenched. 'We need to keep you on this machine for about eight hours,' he said. 'It'll feel like running a marathon. It'll be hard work, but if the antibiotics don't clear your lungs by teatime, we've got real problems.' He had the air of a conductor exhorting his orchestra to pour their souls into the finale. As the nurse gave Magteld her first injection, Dr Houtsma proposed to reconvene at the end of the day.

Sanneke was already at the hospital when I arrived from Adam's school. The rest of the family appeared during the morning. The room was unbearable, with its smell of plastic and its chirping monitors. Magteld didn't care for having her family crowding round her bed, especially when the doctors were with her. This was not how she had scripted her last days. We worked in rotation, looking in every now and then to utter a few encouraging words, as if she were taking part in a charity challenge. The rest of the time we sat in the waiting area exchanging light gossip.

Harsh pure sunlight streamed in through the high windows. Euan kneeled on the cushioned bench, not saying a word, gazing down at the tiny people creeping along the pathways. I wondered how long he would last before somebody had to take him home.

As lunchtime loomed I buried myself in organising the rest of the day. I found a leaflet about overnight accommodation for relatives. Someone would need to take the boys home and put them to bed while I stayed in the hospital, since there was no question of Magteld coming home that night.

The doctor visited again, calmer now, since Magteld seemed alert and bright. She was breathing more freely, though she felt tired. It was just a matter of battling through and taking her rest in the evening. She nodded. Speech was beyond her. The doctor proposed to come back at five o'clock and review the situation. I took it as a positive sign that the medics were happy to let the treatment run its course.

I fetched Adam for his lunch break. There was just time to bring him upstairs. He took in the strange scene with the oxygen mask and the plastic tubes and wires connecting his mother to various computers. After a few minutes of watching silently, he went over to the window and peered out. Then I took him downstairs for lunch in the hospital canteen. Magteld couldn't kiss him or do any more than wave. I promised him we'd return after afternoon school.

In the canteen I kept the focus on immediate concerns: what to eat, where to sit, when he needed to go back to school. Talking in this mechanical way insulated me from thinking about what was going on upstairs, in the room where Magteld lay, beyond the salvation of love.

By the time I got back from the school, Marlies had arrived, completing the family. She was in the room with Magteld. Euan was starting to behave like a wasp in a jar; I asked Luc to take him home for a break. 'He can come back this evening,' I said to Sanneke, who raised an eyebrow and replied, 'This evening?' Then Marlies emerged from the room in a slow dash, her eyes filled with tears and talking about 'the hazy look in her eyes'. And I understood that the universe had tilted.

In the weeks that followed I often pondered when Magteld knew that the die was cast, the ball bearing in the roulette wheel had landed on zero, that she would not be coming home, at least not in this form, that last night's steamed pears had been her last meal, that she would not see the sun set again or sit with me in the living room, our hands clasped together, feeding on pear ice-creams and the life-and-death drama of *Breaking Bad*. That this hospital bed, in this awful sterile room with its disinfectant signs, was where her journey would end.

I went in and registered the watery gaze in her half-closed eyes. She turned her head and beckoned me with a light grimace. I clutched her hand. 'I don't want anyone here right now,' she whispered. 'I just want to rest.' I nodded and went back out into the corridor. I filled the time trying to sketch out her poem, which I had decided would have some connection with flowers, since that had once been her livelihood. I phoned my parents, and Stephanie, who had been due to start looking after the boys the next day.

I went back through the curtain. Magteld's eyes had a different aspect now, a wretched stare of disbelief. She lacked the strength to sweat or shiver. I grabbed her hand and said, 'Shall I get the boys?' She nodded wearily, her eyes soaked with tears. Now she knew, now she truly despaired. I rushed back outside. Diny phoned Luc, who had just arrived at our house with Euan, and instructed him to come straight back out again. How would an autistic eleven-year-old deal with this catastrophic breakdown in the world order? Adam had disengaged from the circle and was staring out of the window. At first I wanted to wait until Euan returned, so the boys could be together in the now imminent final scene. But after around ten minutes I changed my mind and took him through the curtain.

Magteld was lying back, her skin pallid, her eyes diminished to grey slits. Her mouth hung open, her upper teeth jutting out like a shipwreck, as she hauled in the breaths. What must she have been thinking in the time since I last saw her? *Gordon, where the hell are you? I want my boys here now.* I grabbed her limp hand and spoke: 'Euan is coming, Euan is coming.' Not a flicker of recognition. The reiki nurse appeared and picked up one of the hand-held monitors wired to Magteld's body. The number on the screen was ticking slowly downwards. Whatever it was measuring, the message was unmistakable.

Adam came over to the bed and stood sullenly over Magteld. He couldn't make her eyes open or her fingers twitch either.

'Your mum's dying,' I told him.

'I know,' he said, and retreated to the window.

Out in the streets his brother and his grandfather were weaving through traffic, racing against death. Luc and Euan still had to make it through the hospital to the lifts at the back, ride up to the fifteenth floor and along the corridor. Dr Houtsma rushed in, his shroud of affability now cast aside.

'If there's anything you still need to do, do it now,' he said. I told him we were waiting for our son to come, and he pumped a shot of adrenaline into her arm. A few days ago we were hoping he could buy us another six months; now our best outlook was half an hour.

Magteld was forcing the breaths out now. I squeezed her still-soft hand tighter and began chanting: 'We love you, we will always love you, hold on, Euan is coming.' A head of foam burbled up in the pit of her mouth. Her lungs had become a swamp. Her breathing stilled. The nurse, who was sitting by her bedside, waiting, shifted forward slightly.

The curtain behind us rustled and Euan appeared in the doorway, smiling uneasily. All heads turned towards him. I shouted at Magteld: 'Euan is here!' A flurry of excitement, a shuffle of feet on the linoleum floor. Magteld heaved one more breath, then another, wrenched from the brink of the abyss. Her eyelids flickered towards the end of the bed, where Euan was standing. 'She's looking,' said the nurse. And then stillness.

The nurse leaned forward and placed a finger on Magteld's wrist.

'Ten past four,' she said.

In the months that followed I kept returning to her last moments, those two dredged breaths, the final flicker of her eye. Her implacable resolve to have the last word even as death closed its fist. Where did she gain the strength to endure for those extra few seconds and realise the wish she had made in Glasgow, to leave this world in the presence of her three boys? What did she see as the last of the light penetrated her eyes? Could she make out the outline of Euan, his clear blue eyes, his shimmering hair and innocent grin? Did she feel euphoria, or absolution, or closure? And why was it so important to record an image that she had no time to reflect on? Did she think she could take the memory with her?

Dr Houtsma was the first to console me. He strode through the curtain, calm and businesslike, and shook my hand. I mumbled something incoherent. Everything had unravelled so rapidly, like a bundle of hay in a gale. Next came the doctor who had admitted Magteld in the morning and had been due to check on her at five o'clock, half an hour from now.

A nurse quietly asked about organ donation. Thankfully Magteld had made it clear in her last months that she wanted the medical world to learn from her death, and I conveyed this in detached tones, as if directing a tourist to the bank. The medics withdrew, and the nurses dismissed us from the room. 'You don't need to see what happens here,' one of them explained.

Marlies reacted first as we emerged from behind the curtain. 'Has it happened?' she said. I nodded dumbly. We embraced each other in near-mute incomprehension, shedding stifled tears. We had lost a wife, a daughter, a mother, a sister and an aunt. Individually, our grief was unbearable; as a group, it bound us together.

The nurse beckoned us back in. Magteld was still warm, still limp. One by one her family said goodbye and left. Once they had gone I sat down beside her. I had the sense of being on the threshold of death, suspended in time. Beyond the plastic curtain lay that fearful place, the land of grief, and soon I would have to rise and step through it, knowing I would never see her face again, and resume my diminished life. I was in no hurry to start that journey. Magteld lay, calm and attentive and beautiful, as I read out the poem I had promised her. I released the hastily assembled words into the hushed room. It was a relief to see her so still. The struggle had left her. She no longer had to worry about being assaulted in the night by pain and fear. That was my domain now.

After sitting silently for a few more minutes I got up, imprinted one last kiss on her sweatless brow, and went through the curtain.

I phoned my parents; my mother answered. For the first time since I was six she comforted me as I sobbed. Once I had hung up, the nurse came over and handed me the wedding ring I had placed on Magteld's finger on that damp day twelve and a half years ago, together with her watch. It was time to go home.

We descended the fifteen floors, leaving Magteld suspended above us, said goodbye to each other in the lobby and headed out separately across the car park, where it had just started to rain.

13

Funerals in the Netherlands are arranged briskly, in a matter of days. Within a few hours of Magteld's life ending, and with the sun that had risen as we sat together at the dining table still dangling in the sky, I opened the door to an immaculately dressed young man with an expression of studied compassion: soft wide eyes, a polite, conciliatory smile and the air of being ready to listen for all eternity.

Sanneke and I guided him into the living room and gestured to him to sit down. 'Was the lady ill?' he asked.

'It was expected and unexpected,' I said. 'She had terminal cancer. But until the last few days she seemed to be coping well.' I tried to suppress a sob, then yielded to it. For half a minute it was the only sound in the room, which seemed suddenly to have swelled to the size of a cathedral. Then I took a deep breath and we carried on.

The ceremony should last around thirty minutes, the undertaker said. It could be as formal or informal as we wanted. He handed us a brochure of coffins and waited while we picked one out. Magteld had specified a plain box, since the thing was only fit for burning. We needed to decide who would give speeches and what music we wanted to play. There was the facility to display a slideshow of photographs through the ceremony.

Together with Sanneke, I went through her drawers and selected the last outfit she would ever wear. We agreed it should be something decorous and flattering since, as Sanneke observed, Magteld had become 'more vain in her last days'. We settled on a recently bought black dress, with a silver band slung diagonally across the chest and the skirt halfway down to the knee. We folded it, put it in a plastic bag with some essentials, and handed them to the undertaker.

The undertaker asked about dates. Friday would be too soon, I said, since my family would be travelling from England. Next Monday was fully booked, which left Tuesday. Sanneke felt that a gap of eight days was too long. The undertaker phoned his office and asked if there was space on Saturday. There was, and we booked a slot at the crematorium for early afternoon.

I was most nervous about the flowers. This was the one element of her funeral for which I had specific instructions. I sensed Magteld hovering over my shoulder, ready to launch her most withering look if I went off track. She would want hyacinths, I said, and chrysanthemums and lilies, but only a few, or it would look too clichéd. Most importantly, lots of greenery and a loose, unfussy arrangement. She wanted the boys and me to each lay a single stem on her coffin; others could do the same if they wished.

The undertaker would come back on Wednesday to pick up the photos for the slideshow and note our choice of music. I asked him how he got into his job, since he looked no more than twenty-five, a perverse age to be in the death industry. It was a personal choice, he replied; his family was not in the undertaking business. 'I remember when my grandmother died and a man came to the house to organise her funeral. He seemed so kind and calm and reassuring. As I got older I decided that was what I wanted to do.' It was a true vocation, I suggested, a job you had to be wholly committed to. He nodded, handed us his card and went out quietly into the weakening light.

That week my Dutch vocabulary acquired all kinds of phrases I had no desire to learn, but the language of grief clings like brambles. Cards arrived with pictures of flowers and the words *met oprechte deelneming* (with deepest sympathy). Adam's classmates compiled a book of pictures and messages, in Dutch and English, the pithiest of which stated plainly: 'Don't like it that your mother is dead'. Mothers I had only known a few days approached me in the playground and said *'Gecondoleerd'* (commiserations), *'Dat is jammer om te horen'* (I'm sorry to hear that) and *'Veel sterkte bij dit grote verlies'*. This last one has no true equivalent in English – literally it's wishing you strength in coping with a terrible loss. I was grateful for it, since strength was the thing I needed above all. Another recurrent phrase was *'We leven heel erg met je mee'* (our lives are very much with yours) – similar to 'you are in our thoughts', but more vivid because it speaks of shared experience.

I was glad to be busy. I had to organise a cremation, console my children and deal with the gaping puncture hole in my life. Given a sliver of a chance, or five seconds too long to reflect, I would have folded like a shot bird.

I woke in the middle of the night, wrapped in darkness and oppressed by the lightness of the space beside me. Grief surged like a storm-wave and I pumped it out in great gasping sobs. Once they subsided I settled into the kind of unbroken sleep I hadn't experienced in months. This went on for several weeks.

The first time I woke alone I wondered, for a few seconds, if the whole scene had been a mirage, a ghastly rehearsal for the final act. But the vacated bed and the redundant wheelchair beside it extinguished any residual hope. I had prepared myself for the emptiness, but the relief was an unpleasant surprise. I no longer had to concern myself with whether Magteld was suffering, or fetch her medicines and ice-creams from a dark kitchen. All those questions had been settled in the most abysmal way.

Then there was the survivor's guilt. For Magteld the end had been dramatic and violent, and yet here we were, emerging unscathed from our beds. I got up, composing a list of tasks in my head. Adam's school had to be told he wasn't coming in. The wheelchair and all the disability equipment needed to go out to the shed – I wanted to banish all evidence of her illness from sight, summarily. Already I was sifting the memories. The children needed breakfast. I had to call my parents so they could make plans to travel to the funeral. The shopping needed to be done. Time made its demands, ruthless and insatiable.

Euan and Adam had been there at the end, and the shards of their mother's demise were scattered through the house, from the empty chair at the dinner table to the wheelchair ramps, but they didn't mention it once. I concentrated on tending to their daily lives, making sure they ate, slept, washed themselves and had time to play. Life was mechanical. Before they went to bed we sat together in the living room and I read them a story. The book in that first week was *My Dad's a Birdman*, by David Almond, about a girl who helps her father cope with the death of her mother. I'd bought it while Magteld was alive, hoping I could gently introduce the boys to their fate, but fate had other ideas.

I posted her last blog posthumously, headed with an explanatory note and a picture of Magteld at Marlies's wedding. She is smiling, her hair and teeth perfectly straight, a glint of precious happiness in her eye. The responses flooded in. At least Facebook and Twitter enabled me to avoid repeating the wretched banality: *she's dead, she's dead, she's dead.* A few friends phoned; others sent messages, by card or text or online. I was glad not to have to talk too much. Conversation was oppressive.

In a few days I had to rustle up a speech, pluck a few dozen photos from the digital thicket and field enquiries from the undertaker, friends and relatives. I wrote the eulogy in Dutch, as a tribute to Magteld and an acknowledgement of the challenges that lay ahead. For eighteen years she had been the one with the difficult name and the foreign accent; now the baton was in my hand. Thanks to her I had two half-Dutch children and a foothold in another country's culture. Delivering the address in my second language also meant I had to concentrate on pronouncing the words properly, which drew the sting from their meaning.

A life of thirty-eight years had to be compressed into a ten-minute slideshow. From the infant in dungarees and clogs, turning her head towards the camera, to the dying woman, still smiling tenaciously as the darkness closed in. When the undertaker came back I handed over the images on a USB stick, together with the music for the ceremony.*

I had one final request. A friend had written to me recalling Magteld at a wedding in the summer of 2005, just before Adam was born. It was held at a castle in East Lothian, on a long June evening when the lingering sun gave the green fields a copper tinge. Magteld had turned up, plump-bellied and radiant, in a maternity dress pulled from Mothercare's clearance rack. 'She must have been seven or eight months pregnant, and she was so happy,' my friend wrote. 'I think she danced more than we did.' Who else could have dazzled that night as Magteld did, in an outfit that cost less than a bus ticket, carrying an almost full-term baby and glistening with joy? Though I had no belief in any kind of afterlife,

* The songs played at Magteld's funeral: 'Tender' – Blur, 'Yes I Am' – Melissa Etheridge, 'Calm After The Storm' – Common Linnets, 'I'm All You Need' – The Divine Comedy.

there was something irresistible about the idea of Magteld dancing freely among the stars. She was no longer with us, and the human imagination abhors a vacuum. More importantly, if she was invited to dance and had nothing suitable to wear, she would haunt me for all eternity. So I told the undertaker to take her best dress, lay it beside her in her coffin and let it mingle with her in the flames.

The rain that had started falling when Magteld died lasted for three days, and by the time it ceased, her funeral was arranged. I had the eulogy vetted by a translator friend for linguistic blunders, and translated my and Luc's speeches for the English-speaking mourners. On the Friday I went to buy a shirt from a local clothes shop. The proprietor, sensing an opportunity, tried to foist a matching woollen cardigan on me.

'No thanks,' I said, 'I'll be wearing a jacket and tie. It's for a funeral.'

'But, sir, ties are so old-fashioned,' she advised. 'This will really make you stand out.'

'It's my wife's funeral. I'm delivering the eulogy. I think I'll stand out enough.'

From there we proceeded swiftly to the checkout.

Saturday was a bright, crisp day, the perfect conditions for an abrupt farewell. A week earlier we had sat out in the garden with Magteld, to wish Euan many years of health and prosperity. One of the last pictures taken of her shows her sitting in her wheelchair, in the living room, her father clasping her on the shoulders, as if reassuring himself that his daughter was still a person of solid flesh. Now the sun was shining again and the garden was set up for another family gathering, to celebrate her truncated life. The two weekends took place in the same confined space, but in different countries: one in the realm of innocence and hope, the other in the land of grief.

Before the guests arrived Mum and I walked up to the flower stall at the end of the street to choose the single stems: yellow for Adam, red for me and white for the others. Out of respect for Magteld we didn't interrupt the florist's superfluous injunction about keeping the blooms fresh.

As guests began to arrive, Luc and I went ahead to the crematorium. We were led into a small, plain anteroom and drank coffee served from a machine. We sat and talked, quietly and openly. Neither of us felt weighed down by emotion; we wanted to focus on the ceremonial duties after the maudlin frenzy of the past week. It was a blessed relief from being woken in the darkest hours by visions of Magteld in her last moments, her bleached face frozen in a ghastly yawn. We wanted to match the dignity and resolve she had shown in her final weeks.

The dark-suited mourners filed in, clutching each other for support, weeping mutely. The funeral director distributed the order of service and copies of my translations. They tossed the single stems on to Magteld's coffin, as she had envisaged, and retreated to the pews. The plain pine box was on a stage at the front of the room, with the mourners facing it in an arc; there was a screen above, on which her life story was relayed in a series of suspended moments, threaded together by her cornflower-blue eyes and slender smile.

I stepped up to the lectern where the eulogy had been placed, red lines marking the most difficult words and phrases. Two thousand words of prose, crafted from the landscape of memory for nobody's coin. The finest kind of work. The entire span of our relationship, across two decades and three countries, condensed into ten minutes. We met, we fell in love, she crossed the sea, the children were born, she had cancer, we crossed the sea again, she died. I spoke of the innate intelligence that burned inside her, like a fire in a cave, and captivated me. I recalled our first moments together in the hills above Lake Garda; our wedding on a dreich autumn day in Drenthe; the gruelling years in Glasgow as she coped with raising two autistic children, detached from her family. And finally I addressed the illness that had intruded on, and finally laid waste to, her life and led us to this dismal, dignified place.

Luc almost buckled under the weight of his opening words: 'Dear daughter, we have had to let you go.' Then he started to narrate her early life, and the memories revived him. He told of the day Magteld was born at home, on a morning in early March, welcomed by the chirp of birds as they built their nests in the deep-pitched roof. Of how he cycled home in the evening, and Diny would pedal out to meet him at halfway with a tiny Magteld sitting in a basket on the handlebars and squawking with glee: *'Hoi, papa!'* Those days of fledgling parenthood must have seemed as endless and untroubled as the Dutch horizon. How as a girl she floated through life, possessed by a wistful curiosity and detachment: 'I can see you now, wandering around on holiday, looking at flowers and plants and other wildlife.' The boldness and curiosity that she engaged on behalf of her children as she forged a path into the political arena. And the memories forged in those final weeks as her life hurtled to its close – fraught, precious and indelible.

Throughout all this the wooden box sat squatly on the dais, a few feet away, barely noticed by the gathering. Some residue of Magteld was inside it, waiting to be dispatched, but her presence was elsewhere: it was in the words that filled the room and the pictures overhead, and in our minds. It was as if she were just out of reach, on the other side of a partition or standing across a gorge, silently watching. The coffin, with its coating of flowers, was the brutal symbol of that divide. We stepped up to the platform and arranged ourselves around it. The wooden doors slid open and the coffin glided towards the furnace. We clasped each other as tears streamed down our faces. Euan leaned into me, sobbing wretchedly, the first clear sign that he knew his mother was gone for ever. It was the bitterest consolation to know that he could share in our grief.

Afterwards we convened in a side room to consume coffee, tea and biscuits. The solemnity of the service was banished; laughter was no longer taboo. The undertaker came over and discreetly handed me a plain folder containing the paperwork I needed to convince banks and similar institutions that she was certifiably dead. I thanked him sincerely for his efforts; it had been a beautiful, agonising occasion, complying with Magteld's wishes. Presently we would go to the house and drink prosecco in the garden, as she had directed, and watch the children play, and comfort each other in the invasive sunshine.

*

In those first weeks it was as if nothing had changed. Imagine a roulette wheel coming out of its spin: the unwinding isn't apparent at first, until it reaches the point where you start to distinguish the slots and the ball begins jumping in and out of them, finally settling on a number and coasting to a halt, its manic energy spent. The early days ran on latent energy; we were too consumed with the mundane demands of everyday life to mourn, and the memories of Magteld were still warm and nourishing, like the heat from a fading star.

It became normal to set three places at the dining table, lie across the width of the sofa in the evening, and come in from the school scooter run without hearing her voice calling out from the dining room. Sometimes I reached the end of a busy day, filled with shopping and cleaning and changing bed linen, and realised with a pang of remorse that I hadn't thought of her once. The boys made no concessions to their mother's absence: they ate, slept and played on the computers as they had before, and settled down to sleep after a glass of milk and a bedtime story. But the drizzle of bereavement seeped into our lives. Grief was ever present, lapping at the shoreline and occasionally breaking through in waves before retreating just as quickly. I feared it would seize me as I stared at the rows of vegetables in the supermarket, dumbly trying to work out whether we should have carrots or cucumbers with supper, and then cursing myself for dithering over such banalities when the love of my life had gone to the eternal blackness. A few days after the funeral I found an unfinished punnet of mushrooms in the fridge that was past its sell-by date and realised I had bought it a week earlier as I pushed Magteld round the shop. How the hell, I thought as I slung it furiously into the bin, could these mushrooms last longer than my wife?

In June the World Cup began. Just after it started I drove up to a small commuter town outside Amsterdam to interview Rob Rensenbrink, one of the stars of the 1974 and 1978 Dutch teams. We chatted quite amiably for an hour, mostly about football, as he relayed the old tales, honed and polished from forty years of repetition, like an epic poem. At the end he asked me about my life in the Netherlands, and I explained, quite casually, that I'd recently arrived in the country and my wife had just died.

'How long ago?' he asked.

'Two weeks,' I said.

A look of startled disbelief crossed his face. Only then did I realise how shocking it must be to see someone walking around in the immediate aftermath of such a devastating event, apparently unscathed, with the rubble still smoking in the background.

The open wound of Magteld's loss scabbed over quickly; the imprint of her last moments was no longer burned on the inside of my eyelids when I woke in the night. That final scene, when the boys and I stood by her hospital bed and watched her draw her last breaths, was etched in history, already distant, like a picture in a school textbook. Part of me still expected to discover that the whole thing was some malicious cosmic trick. I could not repel the absurd idea that I should keep her possessions in order, ready for the day when she strolled back in the door, a bemused smile on her face, and asked, 'Where did you think I'd gone?'

I saw her in the box of jewellery on her bedside, in the photographs in the hallway, her iPad and the books she would never finish, the row of shoes by the door, the dresses hanging on the clothes rack and the two pillowcases I put on every time I changed the bedsheets. None of it had had time to gather dust. Yet I also had to face a world that constantly confronted me with my loss. I had to tick boxes on official forms marked 'widowed' and 'single parent' and make endless phone calls to banks and utility firms and government offices to extract Magteld from the circulatory system of capitalism. Detaching myself emotionally was my way of coping with the bloodless demands of bureaucracy. I filled in the forms, shoved them in an envelope and dispatched them quickly, as if disposing of them in an incinerator, before the grief could scorch me.

After the funeral my parents caught the ferry back to England. It was a fine evening, and before going to bed they went out on deck for a drink. My father walked over from the bar to the table where my mother was sitting, carrying two glasses of beer in his hands. In ten seconds they would be sitting together quietly, reflecting on the drama of the past few weeks and perhaps feeling fortunate to still be in good health.

Somebody had discarded a tray on the ground just by the table. My father stepped on it. His momentum propelled the tray across the iron deck surface and into a heavy pillar. The outdoor furniture on a ship is designed to withstand heavy storms and makes few concessions to fragile flesh and bone. My father's foot collided with the pillar with a thud that sent him keeling to the ground.

The beer glasses hit the deck, exploding. My father hobbled back to his cabin and into bed. In the morning his foot was in agony. My mother drove him to the hospital, where an X-ray revealed he had suffered a double fracture in his toe. The configuration was so irregular that the consultant invited his students to take notes on it. He had an operation to insert a metal plate in his foot, like a war veteran. It would be several months before he could drive again, and the slight imbalance in his gait still lingers.

My father's fractured toe changed the complexion of my parents' summer. He was unable to walk beyond a few steps or climb a flight of stairs. He slept on an improvised bed in the games room. For the first few weeks he was effectively housebound. One stroke of luck was that I had asked them to take Magteld's wheelchair and Zimmer frame away with them, so they could go back to the Beatson Cancer Centre in Glasgow. Although the chair was configured for Magteld's more slender frame, Dad managed to squeeze himself into it and wheel himself around the courtyard at home. He ended up using the chair for longer than Magteld.

His sudden disability put everyday pleasures beyond reach: gardening, snooker, cooking, boating on the Norfolk Broads. He relied on others for simple tasks such as taking the bins out. Their summer holiday was cancelled, plans to visit us in The Hague postponed. A helter-skelter journey of a few metres, on the deck of a passenger ferry, had thrown my parents' lives into turmoil. It is a lesson learned hard and forgotten easily that we are only ever one bad fall, serious infection or hard collision away from joining the ranks of the sick and dependent.

I came back from the supermarket the day after Magteld died to find the answerphone blinking. The message was from the deputy head of the school we had chosen for Euan. Months of grappling with the special education system had finally been rewarded with a place, and I was invited to make an appointment.

Two days later I cycled through the Vogelwijk, a neighbourhood of wide streets, redbrick houses, lush greenery and elegant restraint. The school was on the edge of this middle-class nirvana, nestling at the foot of the dunes.

I had a sense of foreboding about the meeting. The previous week I had received a letter from the *leerplichtambtenaar*, the council official whose job is to ensure children attend school. I emailed back explaining that Euan was still waiting for a suitable place.

I sat down across a table with the deputy head, sipped fruit tea from a mug and listened as she explained the arrangements to me. Euan would begin in September, she said finally.

ǀ

It was the answer I had feared. September was three months away, and Euan had not been in a classroom since the end of March. Magteld seemed to be hovering just over my shoulder, seeing if I could pass this first test of my ability to raise the boys single-handed. Failure here would mark me for all time. I knew what she would have done: she would have put her foot down, gently but clinically, and kept it there until she secured the outcome she wanted.

I fastened my jaw and said, 'In that case we have a problem.'

I set out the points one by one, as if laying down counters. Euan had just lost his mother and needed support in dealing with his grief. His Dutch was lagging behind, and our family had just been deprived of a native speaker. A five-month break in his education at such a time was unconscionable. And then the clincher: the council official agreed with me that he should be integrated into the Dutch school system as soon as possible.

The teacher listened attentively, without interrupting. When I had finished she picked up the phone and spoke briefly to a colleague. After putting it down she told me Euan could start after the Whitsun break in two weeks' time.

We lived too near the school to qualify for bus transport, so Euan would have to make the journey by bike. I nodded, thanked her and cycled home, relieved, feeling Magteld would have approved of my diplomacy. Or perhaps she would have scolded me for my brinkmanship, because there was an unresolved issue. Euan had two weeks to learn to ride a bike.

Teaching him would be one of Stephanie's first tasks when she started work, a week later than planned and in an entirely changed role. Her job was like negotiating a labyrinth from the centre. She had to work out how to win the boys' trust while making them understand she was not a replacement mother. There was no training for this, and I was too steeped in grief to offer much guidance; she relied on her wits from the first day.

'What are you going to do about this bike?' my father asked when I phoned him that weekend with the news about Euan's school.

'Teach him to ride it,' I said phlegmatically.

It was a bluff, we both knew. I had only a blind instinct that I could make it work. Euan didn't even have a bike. After scouting The Hague's myriad cycle shops I spied a suitable machine outside Sanneke's local shop, a purple and blue Cleveland with a slightly rusty lock and a chain that made a noise like tin cans trailing behind a wedding car, and bought it for the knockdown price of €50.

The next day I took the boys out to the park for cycling practice. Euan wore a helmet, which must have drawn quietly derisive looks from the natives. (Bicycles are a symbol of unfettered personal freedom to the Dutch in the same way that semi-automatic weapons are to many Americans, and any restriction is frowned upon.) Adam followed on Euan's old bike, with the stabilisers still on, which made progress slow and awkward. We managed two circuits of the park, as I held on to Euan and ran with him, until Adam's yells of protest forced us to turn back.

I feared defeat, but something must have clicked in Euan's mind. Over the next week Stephanie took up the cudgel, guiding him up and down the pavement until, after two days, he was pedalling unassisted, whooping in delight as he went. We practised every day, in a loop around the neighbourhood, going a little further each time, and on Monday morning we covered the two and a half kilometres to school in just over ten minutes. Quite by accident, Stephanie had found the ideal ice-breaker.

The Dutch poet Pieter Boskma, whose wife died of cancer at the age of fifty, said:

> Immediately after the death of a loved one, grief is a kind of friend: so long as the grief is there, the departed is still close by. Your grief connects you with him or her. Later on grief becomes an enemy that forms an obstacle to new happiness and a new life. Until one morning you have to say to yourself: it's over now, it's time to make a new start. It's an illness that you can only cure yourself.

I was in the second stage of this process, when the light from behind is fading but the light ahead is still indistinct and distant, and the embers of memory are growing cold. I wanted to get on with my new life but couldn't relinquish the old one.

In those early weeks, back in June, the land of grief seemed like a sanctuary. The World Cup had begun, and the Dutch were in party mood. Orange flags flew from poles, bunting was draped from trees, supermarket shelves were piled up with gaudy merchandise: hats, biscuit tins, scarves, promotional drinks, sunglasses, teddy bears, sweets. The carnival atmosphere erupted when the Netherlands unexpectedly trounced world champions Spain 5–1 in their opening match. The team went on to reach the semi-finals, though they never again hit the rampant form of that first game, and the vibrant mood was infectious. I watched the Dutch matches with Sanneke and Sjoerd and our children, while at home I flitted between Dutch, German, Belgian and English coverage, like a connoisseur. The BBC had the best studio, the Germans the best commentators, the Dutch the best analysts and the Belgians the best atmosphere, the presenters sitting round a table embellished with oversized glasses of wine.

Migration kept me occupied. Magteld had died so soon after arriving that I still hadn't opened a bank account for myself, so every time I went shopping I used her card, as if her ghost was paying for our groceries. The bank staff were prepared to stretch the rules, having seen me both with Magteld and without her. I was learning that beneath the thick crust of Dutch bureaucracy the hearts that beat are still human.

The article Magteld had cut out of the newspaper about *Vlaggetjesdag* was still pinned to the fridge, so two weeks after her funeral I took the boys up to Scheveningen to celebrate the start of the herring season. The crowds consumed the buns with pickled herring and onions as a band churned out soft rock at a volume that strained the speakers.

Her plans were our guidebook that summer. In August

we went camping in Zeeland, in the tent Magteld and I had tried out in her parents' garden the previous summer, as a foretaste of all the family holidays we would enjoy in her country. Camping hadn't held much appeal when we lived in Scotland, but I felt obliged to instil this national tradition in my half-Dutch boys: unpacking the tent, cooking tinned food on a miniature gas stove and sleeping on the ground in a tiny canvas cell, beneath a gallery of trapped insects. We managed to choose the one week in August that deviated from the gloriously warm summer, as slate-coloured clouds closed off the sky and brought in heavy showers and growling thunder, distant echoes of the storms in the Italian mountains twenty-two years earlier when Magteld and I had first met. By day the sun emerged and sponged up the puddles, and we walked down to the beach or took short outings to nearby towns such as Veere, where the Dutch and the Scots carved up the European wool trade in the pre-Renaissance era, and where the Scottish Houses museum stands as a striking anomaly, a sandstone edifice in a row of redbrick houses, all in the Dutch gabled style.

My fortieth birthday, at the end of August, was a pebble rather than a milestone. It was the second anniversary of Magteld's first diagnosis and the start of our year in hell. She had left detailed instructions to her family to book a day out for me and Sanneke at Zandvoort racetrack, the old Dutch Grand Prix circuit. Only now did I appreciate that her optimism and avowed intent, her 'stronger every day' mantra, had been partly a charade. She had lived in the penumbra of death, her mind in hell, staring at the void with that practised look of derision. She was Joan of Arc gazing at the crucifix as she burned, Anne Boleyn on the scaffold: 'By the law I am judged to die, and therefore I will speak nothing against it.' And having resolved to stand firm, she donned a mask that slipped only occasionally, in the darkest hours of the night, when the silence tormented her.

What would she think of us now, I often wondered as our lives trickled onwards. Would she be proud, or surprised, or both, that I'd started using a diary to keep track of my appointments and put up a rota in the kitchen reminding me when to pack the gym kits for school? The awkward truth was that many things had become more straight-forward. There was no longer any argument about who should take the bins out or cook supper or put the boys to bed. It was my job now to be mum and dad, and I simply had to adjust my balance, like a soldier who has lost an arm, and carry on. She worried about me not coping, so I had to cope, to appease her ghost.

The boys did not speak of their mother. It was a truth as hard as knotted rope. They didn't have the words for it. Not so long ago I would have been told that autistic children didn't feel loss, but this was a bogus reassurance, because I had seen Euan stand at her coffin, convulsed with grief. Adam was more phlegmatic, but if he caught me sobbing he would leave the room, unable to stand my pain. We might never sit at the kitchen table and talk freely about our memories of Magteld and the feelings that her loss aroused. I had to accept, without bitterness, that I would have to tackle my grief alone, and that frightened me, because at times it was colossal, bigger than our house, and threatened to crush us all.

On a Thursday afternoon in July, as the school holidays began, 298 people boarded a plane at Amsterdam's Schiphol airport bound for Kuala Lumpur. The summer holiday stretched ahead like a field of tulips in bloom; many of the passengers were holidaymakers who had been planning their trips for months. A phalanx of academics was flying on to an Aids conference in Australia, infused with a different sense of purpose. Others were travelling to see far-flung family members or simply going home, though around two-thirds were Dutch nationals. They would have sat in the plane imagining the days ahead: sitting on a beach watching the sun set, discussing their work with esteemed colleagues from around the world, or looking across a table thousands of miles from home and seeing a familiar face smile back.

None of them would have thought for a minute that Malaysia Airlines Flight MH17 would be snatched out of the sky a few hours into the flight, snapping their futures shut faster than they could comprehend. They would have lost consciousness within seconds of the missile striking: heard a violent noise, gone to take a breath, felt their heads swim and the air turn cold, and then nothing. They dodged the consuming dread that nearly everyone else knows in their last moments; they still had hopes and expectations even as the rocket flew through the air towards the cockpit.

But my second thought was that this was the worst way to die, because it deprived their families and friends of the chance to say goodbye properly. Magteld taught me the importance of that.

During the school holidays Luc and Diny took the boys to Sleen for a few days, leaving me alone in the house for the first time. The children were looked after, the night was quiet and placid, and as I drifted off to sleep the thought rose unbidden in my mind: 'Would it be so bad if I didn't wake up in the morning?' *It won't hurt*, I had told Magteld a few months earlier, and I believed it. But I had also seen the tremendous effort she had made, in her final days, to organise Euan and Adam's new lives. She left detailed instructions to both our families about what support we would need, right down to preparing her parents for the day when I introduced them to my next partner. She would have consigned me to the flames if I let all that unravel now.

Flight MH17 was shot down over Ukraine on a Thursday afternoon. By evening grief had cast its pall with the suddenness of a power cut. Streets which a month ago had been thick with orange banners and jubilation were now adorned with drooping tricolour flags. Dutch newspapers, usually reticent in reporting personal details, published special supplements focusing on those who had gone and those they left behind. In a country of seventeen million people, almost everyone knew somebody at second or third remove who had stepped onto the doomed plane and whose remains were now lying scattered across fields in a disputed land. A stray rocket had made 298 people victims of a dirty parochial squabble.

Television pictures showed how the fields were guarded by men with guns slung over their shoulders. Negotiations to recover the bodies were chaotic; the political map of the region was changing daily as Ukrainian and separatist armies swapped scraps of territory. Rescue workers gathered up the remains, bundled them on a train and transported them on military planes to Eindhoven.

The country declared its first national day of mourning. Millions played their part by hanging out the national flag or observing a minute's silence. Some kind of ceremony was called for, yet there was no precedent for such a mass calamity. And the bodies needed to be transported several hundred kilometres to Hilversum to be formally identified. The solution was simple, pragmatic and quietly impressive. The plane was met by a small delegation including the king, queen and government ministers. As a bugler sounded the last post, the forty coffins were loaded one by one into black limousines. The stately cavalcade set off up the motorway to Hilversum in single file, occupying the middle lane, passing under bridges lined by silent crowds. A few people cast down flowers, their white and yellow petals contrasting brightly with the black roofs. The rest of the world looked on admiringly at the hastily arranged, precise ritual. The procession was repeated every time for several weeks, identical in every detail.

In the grip of national mourning, the Dutch drew strength from their sense of order and the straight line. The next day's front pages showed the chain of cars, evenly spaced, stretched out down the middle of a flat, straight carriageway.

Flags lined the streets; every house seemed to have the same standard-issue white flagpole topped with an orange bauble. I had first seen them on King's Day in April and wondered where the pristine tricolours all came from. Noticing my flag socket was the only empty one in the street, I decided I should find out. I found a small ironmongery store where every inch of wall space was bristling with handsaws and screws and nails and brushes. When I told the owner what I was looking for he vanished into a back room and emerged, a few minutes later, holding an orange-tipped pole and a neatly folded flag. I handed over fifteen euros, cycled home, the long pole balanced awkwardly across the frame of the bike, and added my red, white and blue stripes to the tableau.

My personal grief was disconnected from the national sense of mourning. These people had their loved ones torn from them by a violent haemorrhage of fate as they were preparing for their holidays. Magteld, on the other hand, had known for weeks that her life was ending. I recognised the pain the victims' families described in those newspaper interviews. But I also knew that each of them had their own private grief to deal with, distinct from the collective mood. Grief is an innately solitary thing: it touches everyone differently. Even in the shared context of a plane crash the experience of losing a child is vastly different from losing a parent, a partner or a pet.

The dignity of the ritual at the airport lay, many said, in the fact that there was no hierarchy among the dead; in public, all were commemorated in the same way. But in the private sphere that grief inhabits, the impact of each of their deaths could not be reduced to a fragment of a larger tragedy. It was a complete pain in itself. My newly adopted homeland was a country in mourning, but it was not the land of grief. They were two different places that I happened to inhabit simultaneously.

14

As the months went by, I wore my grief more loosely. In the beginning the twenty-sixth day of each month was a point when the pain and emptiness closed in and enveloped the day like a dense mist. It was a matter of surviving: of clinging on by the fingertips against the gravity of the abyss. As summer ground on, everyone drifted back towards their routines. The disrupted rhythms of work, social life, family outings, sports and hobbies reasserted themselves by a gradual, almost indistinct process.

None of these comforts could temper the sting of loneliness. Cancer had scorched the landscape. My old life had been discarded on the other side of the North Sea. I sat on the kitchen floor and raged in silence at absent ghosts. Magteld's constant presence was not wholly benign; she was a mixture of guardian and ghoul. Sometimes her voice echoed so forcefully in my mind I had to resist the impulse to turn round and check she wasn't standing there. When

I went out to buy clothes for the children I could hear her sharp interjection: *Don't buy those, they'll look awful.* In fairness, it probably helped me choose better.

Everyone in the family had the same sensation of scraping by, of surviving, of living with the dimmers down. What distinguishes the land of grief from the world of the living is the retreat of joy. You go to work, you go to the shops, you read the newspaper, you cook supper, in a series of mechanical processes. I spent the summer working through Magteld's plans partly because I lacked the energy to contrive new ones. I didn't read a book for months, and when I tried my eyes washed over the words without absorbing the meaning. I was incapable of following the thread of a narrative or retaining anything for longer than a week. I felt dislocated in time. The past was a museum, preserved in glass cabinets, while a curtain had fallen over the future.

My doctor arranged for me to see a grief counsellor, who asked if I was coping. 'I think so,' I replied, but in truth I had no idea. Nothing seemed arduous or overwhelming. I was living in snippets. I got up in the morning and rode the conveyor belt to bedtime. I was careful to keep running, drink in moderation and change the bedsheets regularly. My energy was focused on the needs, hopes and discoveries of the boys. I lived vicariously, sweeping the chaos and horror of my arrested life into the corners.

I missed her, I came to understand, because I needed her. When she became seriously ill I realised how deeply enmeshed our lives were. Once when we were talking about the business of looking after her and the children, she retorted in a flash, 'You don't look after me, I can look after myself.' This was, as I recall, shortly after her mastectomy and in the build-up to her radiotherapy treatment, when she needed daily naps to recover from the surgery. We had nurtured the conceit of modern marriage that we were both free to walk away at any time, without pain or recrimination. We should have deduced, from the fact we had stayed together despite all the countervailing forces, that the truth was more sophisticated. Our lives were symbiotic: interdependent rather than independent. It was a choice, but also a strategic necessity. I needed her poise in dealing with officials, her persistence in scything through the sprawling paperwork, her strength and tenderness.

Above all I missed the intimacy. Not just the physical kind, though it would be disingenuous to deny that. In the last months Magteld's rapid disintegration consumed too much of her energy, but even when she became too fragile, we shared intimate moments that transcended mere sex. A warm and gently breathing presence in the darkness, or a soothing face in the dawn light. Waking at three in the morning and feeling an empty space where your beloved is meant to be is the worst deprivation.

Solitude can be nourishing, but loneliness is a corrosive and negative force, a death of the soul that can precipitate the physical demise. When Magteld cried at night in those last weeks for me to come to bed, she was reacting to the pain of eternal loneliness. The difference between loneliness and solitude is intimacy: Solitude – in the form of a long walk, an afternoon spent reading or an hour on the beach with the phone switched off – can be an intimate experience, but loneliness is always alienating.

When Magteld was dying I occasionally wondered if widowhood could be somehow liberating, but after she died this desire receded. The responsibility of looking after the boys knocked any putative romantic adventures on the head. Dating still seems riddled with pitfalls: *We'd better go back to your place, mine's full of pictures of a dead woman.* I didn't want to sit across a dinner table in my best shirt and have to account for the ring on my third finger.

I discovered I slept better when I lay a cushion on her side of the bed to fill the weightless space. At the root of it all was the awkward truth that I was still in love with my dead wife. I read a stack of advice on how to make space for someone new, but I didn't want someone new. I wanted the person I had before, unconditionally, because even the days that ended in screaming rows were better than coming downstairs once the boys were in bed to an empty room. After a row you can nestle on the sofa and console each other with a glass of wine, but my rage now was directed at the universe, and the universe doesn't do nestling or consolation. Or wine.

After Magteld died a friend remarked that I had been lucky to experience true love at least once in my life. That was both a comforting thought and a troubling one. Magteld and I didn't have an idyllic marriage, but we enjoyed spells of true intimacy. Intimacy, really, is the capacity to share the awkward side of ourselves, the parts we keep out of the social media realm. It is the ability to tell someone we love them, without obligation or shame. Magteld and I said it a lot in the last months. In the hospice, every time I pushed her into the lift and the door closed behind us. In bed together, after I had arranged her pillows and helped administer her medicine before collapsing, exhausted, by her side. At the dinner table, when she looked up from her iPad, drifting in and out of deep thought, and gave me a fragile smile. At the same time, I worried that her impending demise had pressed us into a false, exaggerated pastiche of intimacy. Perhaps what brought us closer in those days was not love, but pity, regret and the loss of hope. Were we coerced by the sense of the lights going out and the vortex closing, or did we really mean it this time, and, if so, why had we been so neglectful, when opportunities were abundant, to look into each other's eyes and say, without constraint or inhibition, 'I love you'?

Dr Houtsma had offered me a post-mortem appointment to discuss the results of the autopsy. I agreed without knowing what I hoped to learn. At the same time he had told us that her organs were unsuitable for donation because the cancer had spread too far. Six weeks later Sanneke and I sat down in his small consultation room. Dr Houtsma was as earnest and polite as ever, but his face was more sombre, and I understood that his enthusiasm had been a necessary charade. By the time Magteld arrived in the Netherlands there was little real hope that she would live much longer. He had drawn up a chemotherapy programme knowing she had a scant chance of surviving more than a few cycles. Dr Barrett's warning that she might only manage a few weeks had, for all the optimism and energy displayed, been borne out.

In the last months the cancer had erupted through Magteld's body. Dr Houtsma listed all the places where it had infiltrated: her lungs, liver, lymph nodes and through her skeletal system. The best efforts of medical science had been powerless in the face of a senseless, prolific assassin. It was a heartless story with no redeeming ending. Magteld had been smothered, and finally choked, by her own body. She had been right to distrust it after all.

Sanneke and I sat in the café downstairs afterwards, stunned, as if we had just listened to an eyewitness account of a massacre. We sipped coffee, wept, embraced and went home. We had our answers but no resolutions.

I had promised to gather together the friends she had made in Glasgow for a final send-off. Magteld knew she would die while most of her recent memories, and the people she shared them with, were in the country she had left behind.

When I touched down it felt like a homecoming, even though I was a native of another city and my native Glaswegian children were in The Hague with their Dutch grandparents. Glasgow was in one of its raucous, self-confident moods, fresh from the three-week jamboree of the Commonwealth Games. A month later Scotland would vote on whether or not to become an independent nation. The air was laced with apprehension. In a huge marquee in George Square the city's denizens were gorging themselves on official merchandise at knockdown prices. What Glasgow was most proud of was that it had staged a better Commonwealth Games than Edinburgh, which had been bailed out by Robert Maxwell in 1986, yet I remembered those games with affection, having followed them as a bedridden eleven-year-old recovering from measles, the glistening rain on the television my only source of light in the world. Ours was probably one of the few households in East Anglia that roared on Liz Lynch as she splashed through the puddles of Meadowbank Stadium to claim Scotland's only track gold medal.

The guests who assembled at Langside Hall were a collage of the thirteen years Magteld and I had spent in Glasgow. They had met her at parties in friends' flats, or in the pub, or seen her dance at weddings. She would introduce herself with her given name, always adding, 'but you can just call me Mags'. The gathering reverberated with the name Mags, which stood for the woman Magteld had become in Scotland. Her qualities were still developing in the last weeks of her life; in that sense she was right to say she was getting stronger every day, even as her body weakened. That was her charm, and her tragedy.

Friends and neighbours mingled with former colleagues, carers and school mums, people we chatted to almost every day and others we had not seen for years. One end of a trestle table was colonised by a group of journalists who sat gossiping at high velocity about the referendum. Another table was a microcosm of our old neighbourhood. They mixed with Magteld's fellow carers, who had formed a blood bond from slogging through meetings with experts and officials. In another corner was my family, clustered around Dad, who had recovered enough from his injuries to support himself on crutches and a walking boot. On a small table the slideshow of photos from Magteld's funeral cycled silently on a laptop, giving her a visible presence at her own commemoration. I thought of Luc's description at the funeral of the little girl who stayed away from her own birthday parties, and tried to place her in the scene.

We shared stories that portrayed her as gracious and headstrong, articulate and dedicated, warm and modest and selfless, as a warrior mother who fought tenaciously for her children, a friend, campaigner and advocate. It was hard to know if she would recognise this exalted version of herself or be flattered by it, since it was anchored in our collective sense of loss and regret. In that sense it was a frozen image of Magteld, as detached from reality as the photographs stamped with her cultivated smile. It missed the essence of her, the vulnerability and the anxieties that her battles with officialdom were steeped in. Just as statues of famous warriors are always raised on pedestals, out of reach of the frothing melee, their stern faces set against the sky and their gaze fixed on a place beyond mortal understanding, so we conjured a phantom Magteld from the snippets of her life. Hardly any of those gathered had seen her in a wheelchair or a hospital gown; they remembered her dashing out of the back door to peg up the washing; or walking up the hill to Adam's school in a headscarf, defying the shackles of chemotherapy; or striding into a room at the start of a meeting, a folder in her hand and a disarming look on her face. In a city of statues, this was the Magteld-monument that was hewn in our minds. Would she have recognised it as herself?

Gradually the impact of the twenty-sixth day lessened, like ripples on a pond spreading outwards. The children went back to school, restoring the rhythm that had slackened during the blissful lethargy of summer. Work slowly began to accumulate – I secured my first contract while camping in Zeeland. My Dutch graduated from a faltering command of the language to a more confident proficiency, though my accent would always mark me as foreign, as Magteld's had in Scotland.

It took me a long time to accept that grief can't be rushed. It is a process of adjustment and realignment as the shockwaves subside. It is, fundamentally, a healing process. Magteld and I grieved when our children were first diagnosed with autism. Only once we had dealt with that grief could we learn to love the children for who they were. The insatiability of mass consumerism and the tyranny of efficiency often denies us the space to let things run their course. Everything must have a goal, a purpose and a deadline. By these criteria, grief is a redundant emotion. But this misses its essence, which is that it cannot be reduced to a bullet-point list. My first instinct, to think that we could simply carry on as before with a few minor changes, had been wrong; my second, to push the grief and the awkward emotions out to the margins of my life, was equally misguided. I was in the land of grief, for better or worse. I needed to keep my mind in hell and find my bearings.

During the October school holiday we visited my parents in Norfolk, for the first time since emigrating. In the days beforehand the boys were anxious, but it was a defining moment in their self-orientation. On their return they were able for the first time to anchor themselves in the Netherlands. The Hague was home, while England and Scotland were places across the sea where they still felt connected, but as visitors. 'We're Dutch boys,' Adam said, 'because we were young when we came here.'

A week or so later, Adam's teacher told me he'd started speaking Dutch in the classroom. Until then I had worried the gap between his two languages would be too great. He understood what people were saying to him but was too self-conscious to taste the words in his own mouth. Suddenly he was producing not just words but sentences, and joining in conversations. At that moment I realised Adam had made the switch in his mind to living in the Netherlands. Until then his present and his future had lacked definition. Now the obstacles started to fall away. In November he asked to have lunch at school, an idea he had fiercely resisted up till then. After Christmas he wanted to ride to school on his bike. So far he had insisted on keeping the stabilisers on, as he was terrified of falling off. So I told him, 'If you want to ride your bike to school you'll have to do it without the stabilisers.'

Adam looked up, uncertain. Usually at this point he'd scrunch up his face in protest. But not this time. I took him out on Sunday for a trial ride up and down our street, and with Stephanie's help he was riding to school by the end of the week. I watched him pedal up the wide pavement, under the skeletal trees, his wheels flashing in the winter sunlight, and reflected, with a pang of sadness, on how dearly Magteld would have wanted to share this moment.

Acute pain yields to a dull ache, then to a bruise, and finally a scar. So it is with the loss of love. By the time we came back from our trip to Norfolk I thought I could feel the bruises healing. As I sat with Adam at supper one night the conversation turned to a museum we'd visited together.

'We went there with Mum?' he said.

'Yes, don't you remember?'

He looked down at his plate for a second, pondering. Then he said, 'She was a nice lady.'

The words landed like a scorching meteorite. I burst into tears. Adam looked at me and groaned, then muttered, 'Bloody hell.' Until then I could only assume that he and Euan missed their mother, or thought of her now and again, so it was partly relief. But they still couldn't cope with my grief. Weeks earlier I'd returned from the shops one evening, exhausted, and sunk to the floor in tears, and the boys responded by pulling shut the double doors that separate the living room from the dining room. At first I condemned their selfishness, but later I realised my despair was overwhelming for them.

These occasional glimpses into my children's inner worlds were consoling and painful, like a blast of sunlight through a barred window. My motives weren't entirely selfless, because in trying to soothe my children I was also trying to displace my own grief. I had to accept that they couldn't save me from loneliness. The boys were coming to terms with their own loss, but in ways that were obscured from me. Self-reliance is an overlooked quality of autistic people. I had been waiting for Euan and Adam to share their grief with me, but this presumed that they wanted, or needed, to articulate their emotions as I did. I tried to show them that sorrow was not something to be kept hidden, or a source of shame. I wanted them to know they could talk about their mother when they were ready, without having a clue when that might be.

Time seemed warped in that endless first summer in The Hague. On 1 November, with the thermometer registering an outlandish twenty degrees, the boys and I ate fish and chips on Scheveningen promenade. We sat in our T-shirts and shorts as people strolled by in the freakish sunshine. I yearned for winter to come and blow out this stagnant, procrastinating season, so we could move beyond the doldrums of our grief. It was five months since Magteld had died, six since we arrived in the Netherlands, and yet the light had the same quality as when I watched her being loaded into the ambulance on that frightful May morning.

Exactly two years earlier, as Magteld was halfway through her chemo cycle – bald, weary and housebound by rain and her fear of infection – I had received an unexpected email. A Belgian filmmaker had found a short story I posted online a few years earlier on a Scottish website, Shortbread Stories. I felt mildly thrilled when the site made an audio recording of it, thinking that was as far as it would go, but now someone was proposing turning it into a short film. The story was called 'Do Not Read This Story' and was a metanarrative about a writer being confronted by two anonymous agents of the state. The title of the film was *Kijk Hier Niet Naar* (Do Not Watch This).

It was especially enticing, for Magteld and me, that the film would be made in Dutch. I wrote back and gave Guy Fellemans my consent to go ahead. Over the next few months I kept in touch, signed a contract and mainly waited. The progress of the film was something to look forward to, a counter-narrative to the course of Magteld's treatment.

Magteld had read the story before submission and told me to change the ending, so she had a hand in its success. She was determined to live long enough to see the film. Just before Christmas in the year before we moved, Guy sent pictures from the set where the film had been shot over three days in Antwerp. It showed a monochrome series of pictures taken at close range in a cramped, soulless flat, which exactly fitted the atmosphere of the story. Magteld and I were both thrilled.

But film-making is a turgid process, and Guy was still working on the final cuts when she died. The premiere would be at a film festival in Leuven, in the first week of December. The three years Guy had spent preparing and refining fifteen minutes of cinereel was longer than it had taken cancer to consume Magteld.

I took a high-speed train down to Antwerp, paused to admire its gleaming, intricate station and carried on to

Leuven. Most of the city was built of inoffensive modern concrete, with a few filigree old buildings hidden away in a well-preserved old quarter. The festival was held in a former warehouse converted into an arts venue, with a basement cinema and a capacious upstairs bar. The film captured the claustrophobic, paranoid tone of my story with close-up shots, almost monochrome lighting and rigid expressions on the actors' faces. I had been intrigued by a promotional shot Guy had sent me of the three actors lying side by side on a bed, which had no obvious parallel in the original text, but it turned out to be a creative solution to one of the many puzzles in the narrative. Afterwards Guy introduced me to the actors and some of the crew who worked on the production, and their partners, in the bar. I wished Magteld could have been with us. The trip was the last item on her list of unfulfilled ambitions and would never have happened without her support and guidance. Those memories brought warmth and sadness – that now familiar cocktail of emotions.

A few days later I had a message from someone I met that night telling me in detail about a personal, painful setback. It wasn't the first time this had happened. Since Magteld died I've told the story of her illness and demise countless times. Routine enquiries from strangers at parties confront me with an awkward choice about how far I should go when people ask about my family, or how I came to live in the Netherlands, or where I learned my Dutch. I try to skim over the more painful aspects, but some basic version of the truth is unavoidable. Frequently people respond with their own candid stories of grief: tales of terminal illness, the burden and pain of caring, or sometimes just shocking bad luck. These stories are dispatches from the land of grief, shared in a spirit of solidarity. It is comforting to know it isn't a barren place. I have joined a clandestine society whose members seek solace together, because we alone understand the suffering that sets us apart.

Winter rolled in at last. We made the morning journey to school in twilight and thick coats, and in the afternoon, after a short trip to the park, we huddled over steaming mugs of hot chocolate at the table, watching rain flicker against the streetlights. Towards the end of the month a letter arrived from the crematorium. The time had come to decide how to dispose of Magteld's ashes. I had a list of options, from burying her in a casket to scattering them at sea. This last choice seemed fitting, partly because our memories of her were already drifting towards the horizon, but mainly because her life had seesawed between both sides of the cold, inscrutable North Sea.

After a little rumination and negotiation, I devised a hybrid solution. At the end of the month I was handed half her remains in a plain white cardboard tube and took her home on my bike, in a plastic bag. She took up residence in a corner of the bedroom, in between the clothes and handbags that I still hadn't managed to shift, but home again.

People warned me the first Christmas would be the hardest, haunted, like Dickens's tale, by memories of years gone by and visions of an impoverished future. To fend off the loneliness I arranged to spend the entire Christmas and New Year period with Magteld's parents in Sleen. At home I brought back a tree that Euan had chopped down with his Scout group during a weekend camp. Another small milestone: it was his first night away from us since we'd moved. No longer constrained by domestic debates about the size of the tree, I picked the largest specimen available, a good seven-footer, and installed it in the far corner by the window. Magteld had been a fan of Christmas shops, and over the years we had accumulated a small gallery of wooden reindeers and plastic fairies. The three of us adorned the tree with the trinkets of those days spent rummaging in oppressively lit boutiques, doing our best to honour her sense of balance and symmetry. When it was finished, and I switched on the lights, a vestige of our Christmases past in Scotland appeared in our Dutch living room. The same objects, the paper Santas the children had made in their classrooms in Glasgow, the preserved pine cones and the long-skirted angel with her wand: all were there, just as they had been a year ago, framed by another window in another city, where Magteld had surveyed her handiwork, fashioned by arms that were not yet withered, and we clinked glasses of prosecco.

I planned to spend my time in Sleen sitting by the wood-burning stove with a book in one hand and a whisky in the other, the ghost of Magteld hovering close by, in the house where she had been born. But most of the time the house was too busy. The six grandchildren filled the house with wild, cackling laughter and the drumbeat of small feet on floor-boards. Euan spent two days assembling a mountain of Lego bricks, turning the house into a miniature construction site. And then, on the third day, the rest of the family dispersed, leaving the two grandparents and the three of us.

The boys became restless. They wanted to go home.

And by home they meant The Hague.

The weather was damp and cold and miserable, and nearly all the local attractions had shut down for the winter. On the last two nights of the year Euan and Adam both fell ill with a sickness bug. So we staggered into 2015, drained by the efforts of minding sick children, clutching glasses of whisky and celebrating the New Year twice: once in real time and again an hour later as we watched the BBC's coverage from Scotland. How far we had come, how much we had gained and lost. Magteld had started the year with a trouble-some cough and not even survived half of it; the children had adjusted to a new home and seismically altered lives. As for me, I had achieved my main ambition for 2014 of becoming an immigrant. And Magteld had made it home, to the house she chose, in her own country, in defiance of fate. A dream we had nurtured for years, in harsh and oppressive conditions, bloomed, in the end, for two weeks. Yet as long as my memory exists, they will be etched in my mind as the most precious of days.

15

In the last half-century the rose-ringed parakeet has established itself in the coastal cities of the Netherlands. The bright-green birds arrived in the 1960s as pets, transported from their natural home in equatorial Africa and India and kept caged in the more muted sunlight of north-western Europe. A few escaped and, incongruously, withstood the challenges of the larger, fiercely territorial seagull and the damp climate. They endured the snow-covered fields and mist-bound frozen canals of winter and gradually made themselves at home. Today the population numbers around 10,000, a third of which overwinter in The Hague. In summer their emerald flash and deep-throated chirp punctuate the wide open sky, while at twilight the trees outside the parliament building tremble and chatter as the parakeets hold court, their silhouettes flickering against the streetlit sky.

In the early days, whenever I doubted my wisdom in bringing my children across the sea to Magteld's country; whenever I felt detached or disoriented or weighed down by the task of fitting in to Dutch society; whenever the pressed and manicured landscape made me long for a rugged hillside and a teeming waterfall; whenever, in short, I thought about packing up and going home, I drew inspiration from these flamboyant incomers. People barely notice their dazzling, arrow-like tails as they glide over houses, down past canals and over sand dunes, cackling as they go, singly by day or in small flocks as they retire to their nests at dusk. But I noticed them. They were migrants who had cultivated a corner of a foreign field, adapting while retaining their identity and carving out a niche among the natives. If these distinctive creatures could thrive in the thrawn Dutch environment, what did I have to fear?

One pin-sharp morning in February I was rounding a corner on my bike, having just taken Euan to school, when the wheels hit a spot of black ice and glided beneath me, bringing me down in a graceful parabola. It seemed to happen in slow motion, giving me time to think, in the partial second before I reached the ground, that this might be my last moment. But the momentum was mostly contained by my right shoulder, and the tap of my head against the ice-bound road wasn't even enough to knock me unconscious.

In the few minutes I lay there, four people materialised around me and started competing to call an ambulance. One helped me to my feet; another wheeled my bike from the kerbside; another produced a cloth; a third asked which relative he should call. Nobody panicked. The Dutch instinct for order is a wondrous thing. By the time I was upright they had already formed a committee and a plan of action.

The ambulances were all busy transporting other black-ice casualties, so I would have to make my way to the nearest A&E, which happened to be at the children's hospital. A man named Peter offered to drive me in his Volvo. I explained that I still had to pick up Adam, who was waiting for me in the house, and take him to school.

'Can you call him?' asked another man, who had just got off the phone to Sanneke.

'No, he can't use the phone,' I said.

He looked disturbed, clearly assuming I had left a toddler alone in the house, rather than a nine-year-old with a communication disorder. My head was bleeding, but Adam would be distraught if I didn't come home.

So Peter took me first to the house, where I collected Adam, still clutching the blood-soaked cloth to the side of my head. I checked myself in the bathroom mirror, saw the red streaks down the side of my face and tried to wash them away. We took Adam to school and drove on to the hospital.

'This is a children's hospital,' said the receptionist, barely looking up. 'The adult hospital is twenty minutes away.'

Peter retorted, 'This is an emergency and all the ambulances are out. He was told to come here.' This man, whom I'd barely known for ten minutes, was pitching himself against bureaucracy on my behalf, drawing on another hardwired custom.

The receptionist relented and asked for my insurance card. I thanked Peter, shook hands and went to sit in the waiting room, which was decorated in primary colours and filled with toys but empty of people.

After ten minutes a junior doctor came along, wearing the kind of friendly expression that children's physicians instinctively adopt. He gave me a butterfly plaster and a tetanus injection. I'd planned to go for a run once the children were in school, so when I rolled down my sleeve I exposed my running clothes underneath, making me look like some kind of hapless superhero. The doctor smiled, shook my hand and let me go. I was tempted to ask for a lollipop. I fetched my bike from where it was standing, undamaged, a kilometre away, and pedalled away, feeling the pain swell in my shoulder.

We scattered the remainder of Magteld's ashes on a wind-less, shimmering blue day in early March, a week after what would have been her thirty-ninth birthday. I had arranged to go out from Scheveningen harbour on a fishing trawler and fling her burned dust over the waves she had crossed so many times. Magteld's birthday had traditionally heralded the arrival of spring. This year, as we went to release her, the season was in full spate: crocuses and daffodils lined the roadside, and a week earlier, as the boys and I cycled along the canal, we had spotted two goslings pottering by the water's edge. The afternoon sky was an unblemished sheet of blue and there was barely a whisper of wind as we gathered in the harbour: the boys and I,

Magteld's and my parents, her sisters with their husbands and children.

Scheveningen in March is just emerging from hibernation: a few trawlers scuttle in and out of the harbour, squares of light pour out of the café windows, and the sands are no longer the exclusive domain of joggers and dog walkers bending into the whipping winter wind. We stood on the sunlit quayside watching the long scoop-like trawlers come in, wondering which of them would be taking us out. As confirmed landlubbers we had dressed for the open sea in sturdy raincoats and shoes.

A man from the crematorium was supposed to join us, but as the time drew near there was no sign of him. We started approaching passers-by and asking if they were from the crematorium, which prompted some startled reactions. When he arrived, Rene was instantly recognisable from the camera slung around his neck and the cardboard urn in his hand. Magteld was with us; the reunion was complete.

Our boat was moored beside another trawler so that we had to walk down a gangplank, up one ladder and down another to get on board. The children went ahead, laughing at the clatter of their shoes on the wooden planks. The boat was simple and functional, with two long wooden benches down the middle, a wide gangway on either side and signs instructing users not to wash or fillet their catch on the seats. The Dutch flag drooped at half-mast. I set the tube of ash down at the end of the bench and propped up a photograph of Magteld against it. She was sitting on top of Ben Lomond, hunched slightly into the wind, beaming contentedly, in a picture I had taken more than a decade earlier before the boys were born. The freedom of the hills, the freedom of the sea: it was all the same now.

The vessel with its rasping engine cut through the glassy water as we moved out of the harbour, passing giant diggers that squatted above us on the quayside like armoured beasts, gleaming in the sunlight. The thick ropes dangling over the side of the boat skipped and danced on the foaming waves. Whenever we crossed from Newcastle to IJmuiden Euan would sit entranced by the billowing skirt of water that seemed to hold the ship aloft. It took a considerable force of nature to persuade him to stay still for any length of time, but the majesty of the sea entranced him. Magteld and I enjoyed those crossings, too, for their sense of occasion. The seventeen-hour sea journey was a gentler, more indulgent form of travel that allowed us to bypass the bloodless abattoir of modern airport security. After we moved to The Hague the children made me promise never to take them on a plane again. It was no great sacrifice.

The engine dwindled to a hum as we reached the spot where the dispersal was to take place. I had explained to Rene that I wanted to scatter the ashes in both directions, towards Scotland one way and the Dutch coastline the other. We could see the latter; the former was down to guesswork and the wind direction. He smiled uneasily and went off to consult the captain. It wasn't a matter of where we wanted the ashes to go but where the wind would take them. I knew that, but the symbolism of the moment was more important to me than meteorological concerns.

I opened the tube, reached inside and pulled out a handful of dust. It felt dry and gritty and strangely light. We've all seen those photographs of sand magnified thousands of times until they resemble cocktail snacks, and I speculated that maybe somewhere in this grey powder there was a grain that bore the exact likeness of my dead wife. Perhaps they all did; perhaps the universe had ordained it that way in secret complicity. Perhaps benign forces had laid on the sunshine and stilled the wind, though more likely not, since the reason we were here at all was that a woman we loved had died of cancer at the age of thirty-eight. I pulled my hand out of the tube and hurled the first clump of Magteld's ashes into the sky. They swelled into a small dark cloud, lingered in the air for a moment, then vanished. I don't think any of them made it to Scotland. But perhaps a grain or two did.

Scheveningen waterfront, with its chunky flats and the palatial Kurhaus hotel, slid into view as the captain turned the boat round for the second half of the ceremony. We took it in turns to dip into the container holding what remained of Magteld and cast her to the waves. We scattered rose petals and flung sunflowers in after her, watching their yellow heads bob and drift on the cobalt blue water (the flowers were a last-minute innovation, both to honour her life as a florist and to give us something visible to mark her patch of ocean). The crosswind was against us now, so we had to fling the ashes in a hard underarm sweep that doubled as a goodbye wave. The children hugged each other tightly, leaning against the railing of the boat, their excitement suddenly muted. When Adam wiped his eyes I assumed it was to clear the ash blowing back onto the deck, but then we saw him looking at the picture of his mother. He had connected it with the charred powder being tossed over the side of the boat.

The engine stirred again, and the boat circled the area where the sunflowers were bobbing on the waves. The captain gave three blasts of the horn to signify the end of the ceremony and raised the Dutch flag from half to full mast. A few of the sunflower heads were still just discernible as we peered out, but as we headed back towards the harbour they sank beneath the waters, their part in the drama complete. We took leave of Magteld once more and felt our grief rise to the surface. We embraced, sobbed, clutched each other, sought softness and warmth beneath the rustle of winter jackets. The boat pulled in, nestled against its fellow trawler like lovers on a still night, and we clambered over the metal ladders, up the gangplank and onto the quayside.

Rene led me into the office of the boat-hire company. While we were scattering the ashes the captain had liaised with the navigation centre at Schiphol to fix our exact coordinates, so that we could pinpoint the spot where her ashes had fallen. They gave us a map and indicated a buoy out at sea that we could look to from the shore in order to anchor our memories of this day. Where other cultures weave fables, laced with metaphor and symbolism, around the grand themes of love and death, the Dutch find solace in precise measurement and the permanence of the straight line.

We had supper in a restaurant overlooking the harbour, the kind of place that teems with day-trippers in summer but was now open and spacious. We sat, talked and dined as the light drained from the sky and the flat water darkened. Despite the prevailing sadness a weight had been lifted. Our memories of Magteld were light and insubstantial, and precious, and through these rituals we would gradually uncouple them from our grief, so they could fly up and dance among the stars.

Epilogue

Summer 2015. A year has gone by. The cabinet on Magteld's side of the bed is still cluttered with the remnants of her life: her passport and purse, her unfinished books and beechwood back massager. Her clothes are still in the chest of drawers, right down to an unopened pack of Marks & Spencer knickers that she must have bought just before leaving Scotland. Her wedding dress hangs in a bag by the door, zipped up in a dry cleaner's bag. I don't have any special attachment to these relics, but they're more comforting than the empty space they would leave behind. Her handbags squat in a plastic crate behind the door (whenever she bought one I would raise my eyebrows in mock indignation and exclaim, 'Another handbag?', and she would scowl, in what became a well-drilled vaudeville act). The ashes we didn't scatter at sea are stored in a tube in the corner of the bedroom, a couple of feet from where she used to lie. Physically that's all that remains of her now, but I feel nothing for it. I think about scooping up a handful of her dust, letting it run through my fingers and saying, 'You're not the woman I married.' But I'm not quite ready to joke about it yet.

A day will come when I need to rid myself of these things. Well-intentioned, clueless people keep advising me to give my grief a place. I should get on with my life, I am told. But I am not ready and don't know when I will be. It is the widower's dilemma: the need to cast off the debris of the past clashes with the basic need to preserve memories. Bereavement is a never-ending fight against forgetting. Every time I throw away an item of Magteld's I am conspiring to push her further into the past. The knowledge we must forget, and be forgotten, reminds us of the death that lies beyond death. So for now I ignore the advice to tidy my grief away and keep it out of sight. The erosion of memory will happen in its own time. These keepsakes are my way of resisting that process, of slowing the inevitable decay and all that it implies.

All around the house, pictures of her hang on the walls, moments from her life captured and framed for posterity. Here on the mantelpiece is the picture of her atop Ben Lomond, huddling into herself in a characteristic pose. Probably the wind was blowing fiercely up there and, despite the sunshine, she was fending off the cold. I couldn't entirely appreciate the beauty of the scene because I wanted to scramble down the mountain and catch the end of the play-off final, where Norwich City were playing Birmingham for a place in the Premier League, as we drove home in the car (Norwich lost, on penalties).

She is standing in the doorway of a bus, in her wedding dress, beside me. I'm wearing a kilt. We are sheltering from the rain. Both of us are smiling, slightly awkwardly, perhaps because we're worried about getting soaked or spoiling her dress on the way to the registry office, where we will tie our fates and the registrar will charm the celebrants with his bilingual address and melodic unaccompanied singing. Later we will sit with Diny and speculate idly about how we might celebrate our twelve-and-a-half-year anniversary, unaware of the obscene reality that awaits us.

She is sitting beside me on a large wooden chest (£200 from an antique stall on the Barras market) in the living room of our second Glasgow flat at the bottom of Victoria Road. Euan is on my lap, Adam, less than a year old, on hers. Three of us are looking down the lens of a camera held by a colleague from the newspaper where I work, while Euan chews on his fingers. The two of us are smiling contentedly, but the first creeping indications of Euan's autism are starting to appear, and the ensuing discoveries will strip away the veneer of certainty and control from our lives.

These staged pictures, carefully arranged to project an aura of family contentment, will probably be the most enduring memories of Magteld, and may be passed down through the family when everyone in them is long gone, but do they show any more than the scrap of a person? Where do we preserve the aspects that never show in photographs: the look of passionate rage in the heat of an argument, or the slight but definitive way Magteld twisted her head, turning up her nose, to signal that her disagreement was final? And what of her voice, the texture of her skin, the warmth of her limbs as we lay in bed, the stork-like cadence of her gait? (I didn't keep the voicemail messages as you're supposed to; the only record I have of her voice is the television clip of her talking about cancer treatment.) All the private moments we shared, when the two of us stood apart from the universe: I am their sole custodian now. But when I choose to share them or put them in a book, am I honouring her memory, or constructing a mannequin-Magteld from the snippets of her life?

'We die only once, and for such a long time!' lamented Molière. But in our fragmented age we no longer disappear when our hearts stop beating. We litter the future with documentary flotsam. Bank accounts, letters, diaries, passports, driving licences, emails, shopping lists, blogs, not to mention the slag heaps of digital images. Facebook pages stay online for months or years after the person dies, their mundane jottings preserved like graffiti on a cathedral pillar. But in the end all these things perish too. Memories fade, and those who remember us die too. Paperwork ends up, sooner or later, being pulped or incinerated. Magteld used to enjoy visiting cemeteries and graveyards, and as we perused the headstones I noticed how few graves were tended for more than fifty years. After another fifty years the names were barely legible. A century is barely a flicker in cosmic terms, but it's longer than most of us can hope to endure. Even the celebrities of the early twentieth century are mostly bleached from memory now. As Virginia Woolf observed in *To the Lighthouse*: 'The very stone one kicks with one's boot will outlast Shakespeare.'

Further ahead, societies will disintegrate, languages become unintelligible and cathedrals fall down. Who now can name the foremost scribes of ancient Egypt or three poets from the Chinese dynasties? Yet all these people had the sense, in their time, of being immortal, just as today's writers furiously scribble against the tide of mortality.

In writing this memoir I realised how moth-holed the fabric of her life had become. Without having a diary to consult I would have forgotten how Magteld pulled her hair out in clumps in the bathroom, the sensation of her fingers crawling up my shoulders as I levered her into her wheelchair, or the way she sang raucously along to Janis Joplin in the car (Janis was her trade-off for me making her endure The Smiths). Her intense hatred of whistling, which she called the Devil's foghorn; the echo of her urging me to stop checking my phone and get out of the door. Now and again she intrudes on my dreams – once I saw her walking up the stairs to Adam's bedroom, smiling at me – but I can't summon her, and on waking all I have is a lingering sensation, like the taste of ash on the tongue.

Molière was wrong. We die countless times and say multiple goodbyes, leaving a trail of pain and fear and grief. Some of us are longer dying than living. It is one of the mercies of the universe that we only endure our own death once.

There was no heaven for Magteld, or so we presumed. She spoke of the 'eternal blackness' and nothing beyond. No hell either. I promised her it wouldn't hurt, and I meant it. I laid the spare dress in her coffin as a memento, not in any sincere hope that she would regenerate in some magical realm. After the catastrophe that had ravaged her physical form I didn't want any creator meddling with her again. A supreme being who could permit what happened to her was a monstrous tyrant, not the embodiment of love and justice. If it was a punishment, what on earth had she done to deserve it? Justice must be instructive to the delinquent or it is worthless. If not, was it a reckless design flaw or the bully's pleasure in inflicting pain on weaker beings? No, she was better off staying dead. But my real rage against God flared in the aftermath of her death: when I needed him to make sense of it all, he couldn't even be bothered to exist.

The first-century historian Diodorus Siculus recounted how the ancient Egyptians wrote letters to the dead as a way of retaining them in their lives. These were not sentimental missives but direct appeals to deceased relatives to intervene at the court of the underworld. The Egyptians believed that unkind or restless spirits had the power to disrupt the lives of the living, so the writer would often grovel to the dead person, insisting they had treated them well in life and should be spared any misfortune. Ancestors were called upon to resolve instances of ill health, misfortune or disputes about property. The recipients were not the distant dead but the recently departed, since the Egyptians saw the ghosts of living memory as more influential than those who were long settled in their tombs.

It seems cruel to the dead, after all they've been through, to expect them to perform this kind of mediation service for the living. An afterlife of being plagued by squabbling relatives to sort out a boundary dispute, or decide who should inherit Great-Uncle Albert's antique wardrobe, sounds like a fate worse than hell. But for those of us that remain, the idea has some merit. 'Who could sufficiently praise the acquisition of letters?' asked Siculus. 'It is by this alone that the dead survive in the memory of the living or that people in places widely separated one from the other communicate, even with those at the greatest distance from them, by means of the written word, just as though they were close by.'

Magteld and I began our relationship with letters, back when we were separated by the sea, and when she first moved into the hospice we communicated by email. There is a comfort in including Magteld in our lives, sharing her children's achievements, which offsets the sadness of her absence. Writing to her creates a sense that she is still among us. It's an illusion, sure, but so is all memory. The Egyptians preserved their dead in bandages and lived among them; in our more materialistic world we furnish our lives with the words and images of those we have lost.

Darling Magteld,

More than a year has passed since you left us, and a lot has happened in that time. What would you think of us, I often wonder, if you could visit us for a day? You would marvel at your children, heading off to school on their bikes, packed lunches and homework tucked into their bags. You could fetch Adam at lunchtime; he will break away from his friends and come running towards you, shouting with joy, and you will wonder if it can really be the same boy who was so quiet and withdrawn in the playground in Glasgow. After school you'll take them off to the park on their scooters and smile as they play in the sunshine, as you did the last time we went out together, when you were in the wheelchair (remember the wheelchair? I can't wait to tell you how my father ended up in it and watch you rock with laughter when you hear it happened on a boat, remembering how you loved to tease him about his ferry stories). You can have tea with Stephanie, at our old kitchen table, and hear about the progress she has made with the boys. Mostly you will listen appreciatively, filling her in on events of their early years that have escaped my mind, and encouraging her. There will be more laughter, and knowing digressions on the bureaucratic merry-go-round, though I hope you'll be impressed when you see how nimbly I now cavort through the paperwork.

Later we will go up to the beach and stroll by the shore, the North Sea rolling at your feet, your hand soft and firm, and I will tell you how much we miss you. I will tell you how the boys speak of you sometimes: how Adam reminded me, as we visited a castle in Sweden, of the castle in Scotland where we stayed a few nights while you were recovering from surgery. It must have been a magical time for him, even though you were sick and tired. Euan is harder to fathom, but sometimes he has sat at the table and said things about you to Stephanie, and at school he told his class how you were 'very, very sick' in the hospital. He understands far more than he can express, but you could see that long ago. They have forgotten the pains of your illness; their memories of you are untainted by the guilt and regret that adults struggle with.

I will put the boys to bed and you can kiss them goodnight, so they can look up at you with the undiluted love that sons have for their mothers, and drift off to sleep, happy, memories replenished. We will sit with a glass of prosecco, for nothing else would do to celebrate this day. We will hold hands, and I will have so many questions, but mostly I will just gaze into your soft blue eyes, and see your quivering smile, and kiss your warm lips, and hold you close. I will restrict myself to a single enquiry: how can you bear to be dead? How, when there is so much living to be done and your shadow is present in everything we share? And a tear will rise in your eye and you will explain to me that you are in a different place now, where you can no longer be touched by age or pain or grief, and that this visit is not for your benefit, but to absolve us, so we can go on living without you. You will kiss me again, and clutch my hands, and I will tell you how much I still love you.

We will not finish the bottle. I will carry you off to bed, and slip in beside you under the covers, and hold you in my arms until I fall asleep, and in the morning you will be gone, and in your place will be the indistinct imprint of you that is there when I wake every morning, for all the days I have left.

Yours for ever,

Gordon

Magteld at her sister Marlies's wedding in June 2010.

Acknowledgements

Thanks, variously, to Judy Moir, my agent; to Alison Rae, Neville Moir and everyone at Birlinn; to Ailsa Bathgate for her diligent editing; to Kari Brownlie for the book cover; to Jonathan Pinnock for the website; to Dr Sophie Barrett, Alison Winter-Wright and Dr Danny Houtsma; to Lieke, Anne-Marie and all the volunteers at the Jacobshospice; to my parents, Alasdair and Elizabeth; to my in-laws, Luc and Diny; to Sanneke and Sjoerd, Marlies and Peter; to Allan and Linda Burnett, Paul and Fiona Hunter, Arup and Sarah Biswas, Catherine Edmunds, Simon Stuart, Victoria Thompson, Sandra Webster, Phil Miller, Fiona Story, Robert Hutton-Squire, Jacqui Law, Stephen Sharp, Barbara Gibson, Anthea Chan, Murray Buchanan, Hilda Huisman, Gill Hoffs, Guy Fellemans, Liz Small and Claudia Kusian.

An earlier, much shorter version of this memoir was long-listed for the Fish Publishing Short Memoir Prize in 2015 under the title 'Not the Journey We Were Expecting'.

Special thanks are due to Stephanie Hogewoning and Astrid Lowe, without whose support and generosity at crucial moments this book could never have taken shape.